The Dream Catcher

Twenty Lectionary-Based Stories for Teaching and Preaching

James L. Henderschedt

Resource Publications, Inc.

San Jose, California

Editorial director: Kenneth Guentert
Prepress manager: Elizabeth J. Asborno
Copyeditor: Leila T. Bulling
Production assistant: Carlos Chan

Reprint Department
Resource Publications, Inc.
160 E. Virginia Street #290
San Jose, CA 95112-5876

Library of Congress Cataloging in Publication Data
Henderschedt, James L., 1936-
    The dream catcher : twenty lectionary-based stories for teaching and preaching / James L. Henderschedt.
       p.   cm.
    Includes indexes.
    ISBN 0-89390-339-6
    1. Story sermons. 2. Sermons, American. I. Title.
BV4307.S7H46   1996
252—dc20   95-47506

Printed in the United States of America

00 99 98 97 96 | 5 4 3 2 1

*To those fellow spiritual pilgrims
who have shared their stories and dreams with me
and especially to those
who have been a part of my story and dream:
our sainted parents, my brothers Donald and Dale,
and my loving family Betty, John, Beth, and Thomas.*

Contents

Acknowledgments

The following stories were previously published in *Celebration* magazine: "A Day at the Clinic" (20, no. 9 [Sept 1991]: 330-1); "Going Home" (21, no. 11 [Nov 1992]: 430-1); "Judgment from Within" (20, no. 3 [Mar 1991]: 95-6); "Liverwurst on Rye" (20, no. 8 [Aug 1991]: 290-1); "Never the Same Again" (20, no. 2 [Feb 1991]: 55-6); "Reflections in the Water" (21, no. 1 [Jan 1992]: 14-5]; "The Breakdown" (21, no. 2 [Feb 1992]: 54-5); "The Express Lane" (21, no. 3 [Mar 1992]: 94-5); "The King Is Dead" (20, no. 5 [May 1991]: 177-8); "The Pledge" (20, no. 10 [Oct 1991]: 374-5); "The Window" (21, no. 8 [Aug 1992]: 306-7): "Under the Bridge" (21, no. 12 [Dec 1992]: insert).

Preface

"What is your dream?"

That question has been running through the corridors of my mind like a child playing hide-and-seek—popping up at the most unexpected times, teasing me, challenging me to chase after it and catch it if I can. It all started with Ed Hays' story "The Stranger's Bargain" (*Twelve and a Half Keys* [Easton, Kansas: Forest of Peace Books, 1981]). In that story Satan bargains with a young man to buy his dream. "I'm not in the market for sleep-dreams or even daydreams," says Satan. "What I buy is *the* Dream;…That Dream fuels your life with meaning and a rare form of excitement…If I were to obtain your soul, I would have just a soul, but if I am able to purchase—at a fair price, mind you—your Dream, then I have changed the course of history" (53).

I have found that it is our dreams that give us reason for living. It is the challenge that commands our very best effort and stimulates the powers of the imagination to see possibilities and reach toward lofty goals. Sometimes we reach those goals, and at other times they remain just beyond our grasp, urging us ever onward toward what can be and almost is.

Sometimes, however, we lose the dream. There are the "nay-sayers" who do all they can to convince you that you are on a foolish quest, an impossible pursuit, or a fool's errand. Or perhaps the weight of just making it from one day to the next, when your income does not keep up with your expenses is just too much, and it quenches the flame of your dream. It is my prayer that this book will provide that "dream catcher" that will call back those lost and forgotten dreams; fill you with zest for the pilgrimage; or perhaps energize those dreams that are alive and enticing you to follow.

As you read, consider the wondrous mysteries of life, seeing beyond what your eyes perceive and hearing more than what the ears hear. See with the eyes and hear with the ears of "The Brothers." Let "Under the Bridge" tempt you to consider where, in this world today, Jesus might return. Reflect on what happens when one truly encounters the kingdom in "Never the Same Again." Ask yourself if you can ever go home again after reading the story "Going Home." Discover the wonderful gift in "Liverwurst on Rye." And discover what impatience reveals in "The Express Lane."

In response to many requests, I have included in this book a space for your own journaling with three questions. Do not let these questions inhibit your creativity, but instead use them as a way to get at the stories contained within your own experience. My hope is that you can be like the pastor who said to me, "I really like your stories, Jim. But they are too long to use in a sermon. So I tell my own stories that I am reminded of when I read your stories." That, dear pilgrim, is what it is all about.

It is a joy to once again welcome you as a companion as we continue on our road of spiritual discovery. God speed!

Your brother in Christ
Jim Henderschedt

Under the Bridge

I
T SHOULD NOT HAVE COME AS A SURPRISE.
After all, for centuries persons had emerged
who had special forth-sight about the coming
of one who was to save and bring healing to
the brokenness of the world. Some cultures
called these people "prophets." That is why the news of the
appearance of such a person should have been taken in
stride and, in time, forgotten.

But this was different. It usually happened that one or
two persons—at most a small handful—were given the gift
of this insight and commissioned (as they said) to proclaim
the coming of this person. What took the world by surprise
were the numbers of people who shared the same
experience.

It was a sudden thing and word spread rapidly. Men
and women, rich and poor, young and old, professionals
and laborers were given the "gift" of knowing almost at the
same time. Some had dreams; others saw visions, but most
just knew. They did not know or understand how they
knew or even what it all meant—they just knew.

The strangest thing of all was that those who knew and
those who saw not only included people from all walks of
life and all conditions of life and people of all creeds but
also agnostics and atheists as well—Hindi and Muslims,

Buddhists and Shinto, Jews and Christians, believers and unbelievers. The one who saves and heals is coming.

They knew. They knew when. They knew why. But they did not know where.

Well, this created quite an interesting situation. News about this forth-told event spread with amazing speed. The attempt to determine where it was to take place had political and religious leaders locked in debate. The politicians believed it would have to be the center of the largest and most powerful nation. Religious representatives thought it would have to be in the holiest shrine. The agnostics weren't sure where it would take place—in a secular or religious center—and the atheists didn't care.

Naturally no one could agree, so each one went on his or her own to make the necessary preparations to greet the one who comes to heal and to save.

All over the world, churches and cathedrals, temples and mosques, synagogues and shrines were prepared and adorned for the occasion. And people wondered, "Where will it take place? In Rome or Jerusalem, Medina or Tokyo, Bombay or Calcutta, New York or Los Angeles, Montreal or Sydney? Where?"

The time drew nearer and people gathered where they thought the appearance would take place. Cities and towns large and small were choked with people. Hotels, motels, hostels, "bread and breakfasts" were strained beyond their capacity to provide lodging for the pilgrims, so that, when the day arrived, there was not a room to be found.

As with all things, there were the more conservative, who believed that the healer and savior would not bother going to the political capitals or religious centers, so they decided to stay where they were and prepare for the coming   in that place that he was surely to choose: their home town. But the problem arose that these folk could not agree on where in their town it would happen.

At long last the revealed time arrived. The faithful gathered, candles glowed, prayers arose, hearts beat fast, choirs sang, monks chanted, bells pealed, incense burned, flags and banners waved—but nothing happened. The expected one did not appear.

People remained where they had assembled, for a while. But when it didn't happen, and when it seemed as though it wasn't going to happen, they started to turn away. At first a few, then small groups, and finally large crowds until only a small remnant remained trying to understand what went wrong and hoping against hope that it still would take place. People were angry, hurt, disappointed, and sad. A few blamed the sinful condition of humanity, stating that things were so bad that even God changed his mind. The only way it will happen, they speculated, is if all the people in the world repent. The agnostics didn't understand what had taken place and the atheists were satisfied because they knew it wasn't going to in the first place.

That night, under a bridge, a crowd of people came together as they did every night because this was their home. They returned from various parts of the region to which they had gone earlier that day to beg, dig through trash, wander the streets, and scavenge through garbage with the dim hope of being able to find food, clothing, or protection.

That is how they eked out their meager existence. They were a strange mix of people—young, old, and children; whole and diseased; sane and insane; drunks and addicts; morally upright and depraved—but they were family and this was home. Many huddled around small fires to heat whatever scraps of food they found and ward off the damp night chill while others joined in constructing cardboard lean-to shelters.

Almost unnoticed he walked into their midst. It was hard to tell how old he was. He appeared to be young, yet his face glowed with the wisdom of the ages. His dress was neither shabby nor luxuriant. The pain of those upon whom he gazed reflected in his eyes. Slowly he made his way around campfires and people until he stopped when a young girl stood in front of him. She reached out her hand and he took it gently in his own.

"What happened to your hand, mister?" she asked as she stared at the ugly scars from an old wound. It was then she noticed similar scars in his other hand.

"Some people hurt me a long time ago."

"Does it still hurt you?" she asked with youthful innocence.

"At times. The pain reminds me why I received the scars in the first place."

A big burly man, the one who appeared to be the leader of the community living under the bridge, eyed the stranger warily. After sizing him up carefully, he walked up to him, extended a fingerless hand in greeting, and said, "Welcome. I don't know who you are or what you are doing here and we won't ask. We don't have much, but you are welcome to share what we have." He indicated for him to follow to where the community was gathering to share their meal.

A young man with rheumy eyes held out a dinner roll that he had found in a dumpster behind a plush restaurant. Someone had already taken a bite out of it. The stranger took it, turned his eyes upward, and said, "Baw-ruch ataw Adonoi Elohaynu...." All heads bowed, and a few, hearing familiar words, whispered the prayer of blessing.

Then he started to break pieces off of the roll and he gave each person a piece, taking care not to forget those who lay outside the gathering, being too ill to move from where they lay.

When he had finished, a woman whose face mirrored the hard life she had lived gave him a cup of coffee from a thermos she had filled at the Mission for Wayward People.

He repeated the prayer—"Baw-ruch ataw Adonoi Elohaynu..."—and he passed it among them.

When they had finished, he held the remains of the roll in his hand. It appeared to be almost untouched, and the coffee cup still steamed with the hot dark liquid. He looked at those who sat around him, smiled, and said, "Today, I have come back to you as I had promised. And I have come to bring salvation and healing. Come, my beloved. Let us go. There are others who have been waiting for this day. We must go to them and tell them the Day of the Lord has come."

Prayer

O Lord, I want to stay where it is warm and comfortable, but you are to be found in other places: among the homeless and disenfranchised, the poor and hungry, the sick and abused, those who suffer persecution and injustice. Grant that I will not turn my eyes away but that I will see you in the lives and faces of those to whom I must reach out in your name.

A Pilgrim's Journal

- Where has the Lord brought healing into my life?

- Who has been the presence of Christ coming to me in love?

- When Jesus comes to me to enter my soul/heart, what will he find?

The Brothers

NCE UPON A TIME IN A LAND FAR AWAY, there was a village. The folks in that village were good people. Apart from the normal mischief one finds among the youth and the practical pranks adults delight in, there really was not much wrong. The law officers the villagers elected every so often were more for decoration and ceremonies rather than for the enforcement of the laws. Once in a great while the local jail had overnight guests, but they were well meaning citizens who celebrated with a little too much gusto, if you know what I mean.

The word around the countryside was that the reason why the villagers were able to live together with a minimum amount of trouble is that whenever a problem arose, a dispute broke out, or relationships became strained, the persons involved would take a day's journey deep into the forest to the hut of two twin brothers.

These brothers were gifted. They were able to see deeper and hear more than most people, and so were able to provide wise counsel to those who came seeking their aid. They were always there, and the people had enough sense to take the brothers' advice to heart. It was only the fool who would ignore their insight.

Well, for years this is how the villagers dealt with their problems. However, the time came when the young folks started to question the way of their elders. Just about everything that mattered was challenged. The "old" ways of doing things wasn't the right way anymore. Even the standards—you know, right from wrong—were questioned. The voices and the ways of the younger generation caused such an uproar that the very stability and tranquillity of the village was at stake.

The older folks tried to accommodate the ways of the young without compromising their own needs. Sometimes they were successful and sometimes they weren't. But things got so bad that the only recourse left for the seasoned citizens was to consult the Brothers of Wisdom, as they came to be known.

When this option was presented at a village meeting, the young folks laughed at the preposterous idea. "Just like the old fogies," someone shouted from one side of the town hall. "Why don't you go home and read your tea leaves?" called another from the center of the room.

But much to the surprise of most everyone there, the leaders of the youth who had been appointed to represent them at meetings called for silence and decorum and suggested a caucus to discuss consulting with the brothers.

This pleased the older folks. They saw it as a sign of hope that the young folks might be gaining some insight. At the same time, the rank and file of the younger ones were set a buzz with bewilderment. A few even thought they were being "sold down the river."

Each side retired to its respective meeting chambers where the issue of consulting the Brothers of Wisdom was discussed.

The room in which the elder citizens met was rather quiet. But the other one was filled with angry shouts of displeasure at the appointed leadership. Some called for their impeachment, and a few even went so far as to suggest exile.

But the furor diminished when one young man stood to speak. He was tall and strong. Many looked upon him as their leader among leaders.

"Fellow citizens, hear us out. We know what you are thinking, and many of you have a right to feel betrayed. But our intent is not to abandon our cause nor is it to give into the way of the old. This is the chance we have been waiting for. Your leadership places no confidence in the wisdom of the brothers. But for years, more years than many of us even know, the ways of our village were determined by the word of those two who live in their hut in the forest. Now is our chance to wrest their power from them. We suggest that a delegation representing both sides be authorized to go to consult with the brothers. We will play along until that moment when we will be able to reveal them as frauds, destroy the confidence the old folks have in them, and assume complete authority in the governing of our village."

This was met with cheers and shouts of affirmation.

And so it was that the delegation was appointed, and on the agreed upon day, they set off on their day's journey into the forest to the hut of the Brothers of Wisdom. The streets were lined with well-wishers. The elderly, completely unaware of the intended deception, were elated at the youth's enthusiasm.

The path they followed was well worn after the years of use. The younger members of the delegation were amazed at how well maintained is was and surprised at how often it must have been used to remain so clearly defined. They observed among themselves that it was high time to end this practice of placing so much authority in the hands of two men who did not even live in their village.

About mid-morning of the next day, after spending the night in a clearing around a campfire, they arrived at the hut. That is exactly what it was: a hut, a hovel of sorts that was in dire need of repair. The youth observed among themselves that not much could come of this since the brothers did not even have enough sense to keep their home in good shape.

One of the younger members, the wife of the spokesman for the leadership, was about to knock on the door when a voice called from inside. "Come in. My brother and I have seen and heard you coming. We have been waiting for you."

She pushed the door open. It creaked on rusty hinges and swayed a bit indicating that its mooring was no longer stable.

It was dark inside the hut. A table stood in the shadows of the small room and behind it were seated the brothers. At least the group surmised they were the brothers for the room was so dark that their features were not distinguishable. A fire smoldered in the fireplace casting dark dancing shadows across the room. Only the elders were at ease. They had been here before. But there was something spooky about it to the young folks.

Everyone stood in silence waiting for someone else to start the proceedings. Not able to stand the silence any longer, one of the representatives of the youth started to speak. "We have come...."

"We know why you have come," the voice from the brother on the left interrupted. "We have heard what is in your heart and seen what is in your soul. You have come because of a disagreement among your elders and your youth. At least that is why you say you have come. You have really come, however, to prove my brother and I to be charlatans so that you can take complete control of your village."

The elders, stunned by the announcement, turned in anger toward their companions. "Is this true?" they demanded. "Would you deceive us like this?"

The accused tried to respond, but they were so flustered that they could say nothing coherent.

"It matters not," the other brother said as he shifted slightly in his chair. "You have come seeking wisdom and whether your intentions are noble or ignoble, you will leave with what you have come to receive. My brother has seen the light and the darkness that is within you. You all possess it—both young and old. You have not yet learned how to mingle the light you both possess so that the darkness within you is something you will not be able to overcome."

A movement from the other brother indicated that he was ready to speak. "And my brother has heard the music within your hearts. It is both harmonic and discordant. You have not yet learned how to combine the harmony so that the discords have no chance of drowning it out."

It was hard to determine who spoke next. Perhaps they spoke together. "The elders seek to preserve things the way they are while the youth hunger for new things and new ways. Both can learn from each other. One way is not always all right nor is it all wrong. The light must hold back the darkness, and the harmony must overpower the discordant.

"We have seen and heard so much more. But that must be saved for another time. For now, if you are able to find the way to discover the light and harmony in each other you will find the way to once again bring peace and tranquillity to your village."

The elders heard the wisdom and talking among themselves decided to return to the village and tell their citizens what the brothers said, and the youth, stunned by what they heard, decided the same.

The wife of the spokesman of the youth leadership was overcome with awe. "You possess amazing wisdom and insight," she said. "I would give anything to have your eyes and ears so that I could see the sights and hear the sounds of beauty that surround me every day."

There was a movement from behind the table. A hand reached out, and suddenly a flame from an oil lamp burning so dimly that it could not be noticed erupted, filling the area with light. The one who turned up the wick drew the lamp closer to himself. "And we," he said, "would give anything to have your eyes to see what you see and your ears to hear what you hear."

The light from the lamp reflected two snow-white eyes that looked deep into the hearts of the people. "You see, I am blind, and my brother is deaf."

And so it was that the village was returned to a state of peace and tranquillity, and a whole new generation of villagers walked the path and sought the counsel of the Brothers of Wisdom until a number of years later some young folks again started to question the way of their elders.

Prayer

I see but am not able to perceive. I hear but do not understand. I am so much a part of the worldly kingdom and have not developed the sensitivity to yours, gracious God. When others give evidence of spiritual maturity, I shut them out because I am either suspicious of their motives or jealous of their relationship with you. Be patient with me, Lord, and send your spirit that I may develop the sight and the hearing of one who loves and serves you. Amen.

A Pilgrim's Journal

- When you listen with the ears of the spirit and see with the eyes of the spirit, what do you perceive and understand?

- In what ways may you have been deceitful in your spiritual relationships with Christ and others?

- Look deep within your heart. What do you see?

The Dream Catcher

THE FOLKS IN DUSTY GULCH DIDN'T PAY much attention to the battered old wagon that stood in front of the Wells Fargo Bank.

They had grown accustomed to the road shows that passed through town. This wagon was just another in a long string that stopped off with the hopes of leaving behind a few bottles of "Miracle Cure" and taking away enough money to have made the stop profitable.

Many of the wagons were fancy—painted in gold leaf and brilliant colors—to go along with the glitter and glow of the "show" and the "product." But this one looked as though it was nearing its last mile. The paint had pealed off long ago, and the springs sagged about as low as the back of the ancient horse that was tethered nearby.

And the horse was a sorry-looking beast. Patches of hair had fallen out, leaving bald spots all over its sides and back. Its tired old legs bore the scars of many sores. A swarm of flies hovered over its head like a flock of circling vultures. Sad watery eyes peered over the top of the tattered feed bag in which its nose was buried.

All morning long people passed by the wagon hardly giving it a second glance. Usually, when a new wagon rolled into town, a tide of excitement would begin to wash over the good citizens of Dusty Gulch. There wasn't much to entertain the folks in town—a dance now and then, a church dinner, and the Twin Post Saloon for the men. But the presence of this wagon did not generate the same enthusiasm. As hungry for a break in their monotonous living as they were, this did not hold much promise for them.

And, where was the barker? By the time the folk started to stir, the barker would be seen walking up and down the plank sidewalk announcing his show and posting signs. Sometimes the barker would take the feature of his show along with him to "tease" the people. It might be a strong man who would bend an iron bar or a contortionist woman who bent over backwards in such a way that the small crowds of people would "ooh" and "ah." It was most unusual that the barker was not to be seen. All was peaceful and quiet, and the people passed and didn't give the rickety wagon a second glance.

At about noon some activity could be heard inside of wagon. At first is was just the stirring of someone, as though rising from a long sleep. But then the stirring grew louder and louder. In fact, there was quite a commotion with a lot of hammering and sawing and stomping and muttering. The old wagon rocked on what was left of its springs like an anchored ship being tossed on angry waters. This went on for nearly an hour. And then all was quiet once again.

The noise did do one thing though: it gathered a small crowd of people. It was a most curious thing. They wondered what was going on inside. Was there going to be a show? What kind of strange surprise did the wagon hold?

When the clamor ceased and the rocking subsided, the people waited. But nothing happened. Just when the expectant audience started to break up, the stillness was shattered with the sound of a blast from a cannon. Men fell to the ground, women screamed, little girls cried, and wide-eyed boys said "Wow!" A huge puff of white smoke billowed from the back of the wagon. The only one in town who didn't react was the old nag, who went on munching oats. It was either stone deaf or so used to the event that it no longer reacted.

The commotion drew a small group of men out from the saloon. A couple appeared to already have had one too many drinks. They stood together, off to the side, to see what was going to take place.

After the smoke cleared, the men got to their feet, and the screaming stopped, and a canvas was unrolled. It fell from the top of the wagon and covered most of the side facing the people. Many patches held the ancient billboard together. In its day it must have been magnificent.

Just enough of the paint remained for people to get a hint at what mystery the old wagon contained: Professor Needlebaum's Amazing Feats of Prestidigitation and the Amazing Dream Catcher.

And down on the bottom a small handwritten piece of cardboard was attached. It read, "Showtime 1:00 p.m."

The canvas once contained some elaborate and festive illustrations. But all that remained were a few fuzzy outlines and some faded colors.

The people in the small crowd that had seen these strange happenings traded expressions of excitement. Something was going to happen that will bring some variety into their mundane lives. One small lad shouted, "Oh boy, a magic show. I like magic!" A small gathering of girls looked at one another, covered their mouths, and giggled.

The clock in the tower on the town hall stuck the quarter hour. It was 12:15. Forty-five minutes remained, giving the families of Dusty Gulch enough time to get a quick lunch before the show began. And so they dispersed, each one going his or her own way, determined to be back at one o'clock sharp.

For some people the time passed slowly. Others made a point not to go too far away—close enough to keep an eye on things to make sure the show would not start ahead of time without them. One or two of the younger tikes played in the street near the wagon. They were going to get a good place to stand to watch the show.

A few minutes before one, the crowd once again gathered. It was larger this time. Friends and family carried the news to those who were not present for the previous events. The clock's minute hand inched toward the vertical position at a snail's pace. At long last, it reached the "twelve," and the loud chime sounded its single note.

The peal had hardly died before, with a thunderous crash, the whole side of the wagon fell outward. The young people toward the front ran back a few paces for fear that the rickety old wagon would topple on them. Something prevented that from happening, and the part of the wagon that had separated itself stopped falling and was held by some invisible force in such a way as to become a stage.

The voices in the audience fell silent. The show was about to begin.

Curtains that covered the back of the wagon rustled and parted. At first the crowd stared at the sight before them. But then, a tittering started in the back, and then laughter broke out.

Professor Needlebaum was a short, squat man. His wide girth gave the impression that he was about as round as he was tall. A crooked grin, coupled with a mischievous twinkle in his eyes, made it difficult to take him seriously. On top of his head stood a battered old top hat, and tufts of gray hair stuck out from the bottom of the hat as though charged with static electricity. Eyebrows so bushy that they seemed to join at the center of his brow shaded his eyes, and glasses were perched on the end of a nose that looked like he drank more of the "snake oil" than he sold.

His suit was stylish—for about three generations ago. Neither his formal jacket nor his vest were able to be joined . The baggy trousers had not even the slightest trace of a crease, and package twine was substituted for shoelaces.

"Ladies, gentlemen, and children of all ages," his voice rang out.

Silence immediately overtook the people. The laughter ended abruptly. The voice did not fit the person. It was clear and strong and commanded attention.

"What you are about to see will astound you. Never before have you had the opportunity to be amazed with feats so unbelievable. You will not believe your eyes. So, I invite you to pay close attention and give your undivided attention because the hand is indeed quicker than the eye."

With amazing speed and agility the strange character on the stage threw his hands out to his side, rotated his wrists in a circle three times, and snapped his fingers. White puffs of smoke rose from the palms of his hands, and when the smoke disappeared, a white dove was perched on one finger of each hand.

The audience liked that. They clapped and cheered.

But one small boy, about twelve years of age, walked up to the stage. "I know how you did that," he said to Professor Needlebaum. "You didn't just pull them out of the air. Those birds were hidden in your…"

"Say, little boy," the Professor interrupted, "isn't that your mother I hear calling you? Why don't you just run along, and keep going until I tell you to stop."

The people laughed as the lad slowly walked back to where he had been standing.

"Now, as I was saying," the Professor continued, "you must watch everything very closely because if you don't," the doves walked to the center of the palms of his hands, and with great force he brought his hands together. When he opened his hands, the doves were no longer there.

Sounds of delight radiated from the crowd. But the same young boy stepped forward again and said, "Mister, I know what you did with those birds. You didn't make them disappear. When you brought your hands together, they..."

"Say, little boy," the magician countered, "I have an idea. Let's play a game."

The boy beamed broadly. "Okay! What shall we play?"

"How about the game called 'Quaker?'"

"'Quaker?' How is it played?"

"Well, you keep quiet. When you talk, you lose."

Knowing he had been fooled, and embarrassed by the laughter of the others, the boy hung his head and returned to his place.

The show went on. The Professor amazed the people. The boy tried to explain how the Professor performed his magic tricks, and the crowd was amused.

After having produced a live rabbit in the arms of a surprised girl, the strange little man walked to the front of the stage. "Boys and girls, ladies and gentlemen," he said, "these amazing feats of slight of hand have amused you and amazed you. These marvelous miracles of magic that have been gathered from all corners of the world stagger the imagination. But none of these illusions can compare with what I now hold in my hand."

He held his right hand, closed around an object, high above his head. "Behold," he announced as he slowly opened his hand, "the Dream Catcher!"

A veil of silence covered the crowd until someone near the back snickered. Soon, as though it was being passed from person to person, the whole crowd was laughing, hesitatingly at first but soon boisterously.

"Hey mister," it was the annoying kid again, "my ma has one of them things hanging in our kitchen only it don't catch dreams. It catches flies."

19

Now everyone was laughing as hard as they could. Men and women wiped tears from their eyes; children were bent over with laughter.

Without the slightest sign of annoyance, Professor Needlebaum waited for the laughter to subside. He held the silver cylinder for everyone to see. It was three inches long and about one inch in diameter. It did indeed look like the container for strips of fly paper that hung in most, if not all, kitchens in Dusty Gulch.

"I know it does not seem like much," he continued after the last laugh was heard, "but behold…."

He pulled a small silver thread that hung from the bottom of the tube. What appeared caused the crowd to move a step closer. The silver filaments that stretched from the small container were as thin as strands of hair and, like the cylinder from which they came, bright silver. The slight breeze that blew caused the threads to move against each other and produced a sound unlike that ever heard before. It was from another world.

"What does it do?" someone called from the midst of the crowd that was once again captivated by the Professor's power.

"It catches dreams."

"Why would you ever want to catch a dream?" a woman near the front asked.

"Why?" the professor countered. "The answer to that is obvious. There are certain dreams we should keep."

One of those who had too much to drink nudged the fellow standing next to him. "Hear that, Zeke? Maybe I ought to buy me one of them there dream catchers if it can hold onto them. I had a dream about the schoolmarm last night I wouldn't mind holding onto."

His comrade snickered knowingly. But a pretty young woman on the other side of the crowd blushed deeply and turned away. A couple of the men winked wickedly at the one who had caused the embarrassment.

With a commanding voice, the professor silenced the ribald mirth. "Enough! I hope you're not too drunk to understand. You are talking about your dreams, the sometimes twisted journey of your mind when control over it is released by sleep. This does not capture your dreams. It captures your *dream*."

Many people appeared to be puzzled.

"Let me explain," he continued. "All of us dream when we sleep. Some dreams we remember"—more chortles from the side—"and many of them we don't. Sometimes these dreams reveal something about ourselves. But that is not what I am talking about. What I am referring to is your dream. All of you have a dream. Your dream is your reason for being; it is that which drives you forward. Your dream is you.

"You, there," he said, pointing to the tipsy man who made the comment about his nocturnal dream, "your dream is that some day you will meet a woman whom you can truly love whom you shall marry and with whom you shall have children."

The wry smile on the man's face disappeared. His eyes avoided contact with those around him. He solemnly looked at the tips of his dusty boots.

"And you," this time in the direction of the schoolmarm, "your dream is that the folks of this town will take you seriously and will bring their children to you because you are a good teacher and your heart's desire is to help develop young minds."

Again the woman blushed but this time with pleasure that someone was able to say how she felt.

"Your dream," looking in the direction of a matronly woman, "is to be able to provide care for the health of the people in your community. You want to be a nurse more than anything in the world."

"And you, young man," this time to the lad who knew all the tricks, "someday you want to do something that will help people to live with one another so that they will love each other and not cause harm any more.

"You don't want to lose your dream. To lose your dream is to lose who you are. That is why this Dream Catcher is so important for you. It will help you to hold on to your dream. Listen to the sound these silver threads make when they touch each other." He shook the strange instrument ever so slightly. "There. Can you hear it? It is singing the song of your dream. If your dream should ever leave, this will sing the song and attract your dream. And in the quiet longing of your soul, your dream shall return. So come one, come all. Just step right up and take home your very own Dream Catcher."

One burly gent shouted from the crowd, "And just how much are you selling your amazing Dream Catcher for?"

"How much?" Professor Needlebaum responded. "*How much*? Do you think I could put a price on something as important as this? Do you think you can pay to save your dream? How misguided you are! I could not put a price on something as important as this. What it costs is your trust, your faith, your own desire to save your dream. What it costs is to believe that without it you could lose that very thing that makes you uniquely you."

At this point many people shook their heads and started to walk away. Others laughed as they turned to go about their business. "You've got to say one thing," someone was heard saying, "he did put on a good show."

A small handful of people did queue in front of the stage and walked away with one of Professor Needlebaum's amazing Dream Catchers.

Later that afternoon, all was quiet around the old battered wagon. The stage had been drawn up, the banners furled, and the canvas rolled. The old flea-bitten nag continued to gaze as it munched on its oats. Professor Needlebaum's work was over.

Early the next morning, just as the light of dawn parted the sea of night, before any of the town folk had ventured outside, the wagon, now hitched to the tired old beast, started to move down the street. Professor Needlebaum, his coat collar drawn up to ward off the morning chill, sat in the driver's seat and held the reins in his hands. A slow and tired "clip clop" sounded as the old horse tugged the burden to which it was attached. The Professor held the reins, not to direct his steed, for it knew where it was going—to the next town—but simply to assure it that he was there.

About a mile or so out of town, a young boy stood by the side of the road. Professor Needlebaum pulled on the reins and stopped the wagon long enough for the lad to climb aboard. It was the youthful heckler.

"Well, Pop, how did we do?"

With a sigh, the Professor turned to the boy. "We saved a few dreams, son. We saved a few dreams."

Prayer

Lord, I have a dream. It defines who I am and what I live for. But why am I willing to abandon it when tempted by the empty promises of the world? Your kingdom is a part of that dream, but I am often too willing to release it for immediate pleasures. When the evil one comes to me, he wants my dream because he knows that when he possesses it, I am the one who is truly possessed. Help me to hold onto the dream, and to long for its realization, and when it does come to pass, may there be another dream for without it one surely dies before their time. Amen.

A Pilgrim's Journal

- What is it that you truly live for?

- Has your dream been fulfilled, is it in the process of being fulfilled, or is it too far beyond your grasp? What is keeping you from realizing your dream?

- Create a statement that describes your dream.

When the Job Is Done

RAN AND LARRY GILBERT REMEMBERED sitting on the same sofa opposite their pastor not too many months ago. Then, as now, they were held in the icy grip of the unknown. And then, as now, long periods of silence broke their conversation into fragments.

Pastor Vincent was lost in his thoughts. He felt responsible for Fran and Larry being here before him again. A wave of guilt passed over him as he remembered the trials that this wonderful couple had to endure merely because he had given them a challenge nearly a year ago— a challenge which they accepted and at which they worked diligently.

He remembered the day he met with them in their home. A number of times they had mentioned to him that they wanted to become involved in some kind of community service that would help to ease the suffering of the poor and needy. When he realized that they were serious and would be persistent until he helped them find an outlet for this calling, he took them on a walking tour in the community that surrounded St. Bartholomew's Church.

That was an emotional and moving afternoon. The Gilberts were shocked at the number of homeless people who slept in doorways and alleyways and at the few sleeping right in the middle of the sidewalk. It was impossible to tear one's eyes away from the empty stares that were rooted in abject poverty. At times the stench of human waste was overwhelming when they walked past areas used as public toilets. But what really tore at the hearts of Fran and Larry was the evidence of hunger and the absence of nourishment and nutrition.

Later that day, after they returned to their comfortable home in the suburbs, they fought the confining walls of helplessness that usually followed an exposure to so great a need. They talked about how nothing is usually done because the scope of the need is so overwhelming. Though it would only begin to scratch at the surface of the problem and the need, Larry and Fran decided to start the wheels turning to open a "Soup Kitchen" in the fellowship hall of St. Bartholomew's. Over the following weeks and months they had succeeded in gathering the support of other neighboring congregations, developed a work force, solicited contributions from businesses in the area, and finally had a thriving ministry going that saw that the poor and homeless were able to have at least one good meal a day. A big hurdle turned out to be convincing volunteers that these people had to eat on Saturdays and Sundays as well as every other day of the week.

But, it was not all smooth sailing. They were not very long into the project when opposition started to become evident. "We don't mind you wanting to feed the poor— God knows, they need it—but do it somewhere else than in our church. Who's going to pay for the heat and the electricity? Besides, we have a nice building, and they might abuse it." The voices of the multitude who willingly contributed to keep involvement away from their doorstep were heard loud and clear.

Fran and Larry did not have an easy time of it.

Finally, the silence was broken. Fran spoke. "Pastor, we feel so bad that we created so much trouble for you."

The musing cleric was startled by Fran's statement. "You feel bad for me? It is I who have had sleepless nights. I am the one who 'stacked the deck' when we toured the neighborhood."

Now it was Larry's turn. "Maybe so. But we walked into it with our eyes open. We knew that not everyone would approve. It's just that, well, it's just not fair that you had to take all that flack from some of the people, the powerful people. They made life difficult for you for quite some time."

"Yes, it is unpleasant. But I am convinced that we are doing the right thing. Besides, I firmly believe that God gives us strength to endure hardships. It's just not fair, that's all. I admire the both of you for sticking with it and creating a ministry that is now self-supporting. I am proud of you."

Fran took a deep breath. When her pastor looked at her, she lowered her eyes. "That is why we asked to see you this evening, and that is why we feel so guilty."

Pastor Vincent was puzzled. "I don't understand."

Larry picked up where his wife left off. "Well, like you said, the 'soup kitchen' is operating on its own. There is a good board of directors, and we have plenty of people who are willing to work and help. Oh, we have to be honest and confess that there were times when we wanted to throw in the towel and call it quits. We just about had it with some of those folks who like to be seen in church but wouldn't be caught dead near the needy. Many times I had to ask forgiveness for how I felt toward those people."

Pastor Vincent laughed. "You're not alone." Tapping his fist against his breast, he said, "My sin. My sin, too."

Larry smiled. "Fran and I decided that we will be pulling back now and letting the board of directors take over. We will still serve on the board and help out any way we can."

"Good, you deserve a rest," their pastor exclaimed.

Nervously, Fran continued. "That's just it. Larry and I were praying about that. We have tried to justify backing away because we did our job, and now it is on its own. We have been staying after the services and placing our concerns before God. We have even set aside time here at home to pray and meditate."

"Yes," Larry picked up, "and we feel that we have an answer to our prayers."

Pastor Vincent sat forward. This was interesting. It was exciting.

"Many of the people we feed do not have any homes. The winter months are coming and that means it will be getting cold again. Fran and I were appalled last year to discover the number of deaths due to hypothermia."

"We took a good look at the situation," Fran said, "and realized that there are eleven churches in the area where the homeless congregate. All of them are heated during the winter, and all of them are locked up tight at night."

Larry sat forward on the sofa, "We thought that we would like to challenge the churches to open their doors and provide space on cold nights where people can find shelter from the harsh weather. We would like to—"

Pastor Vincent started to laugh. "Oh, no. Here we go again."

Prayer

Lord, when Elijah was hiding in a cave you went to him and asked a simple question. "What are you doing here?" you asked. Sometimes you ask that of me, and I ask it of myself. Help me to know what it is that will fulfill my role as a servant in your kingdom. And when the job is done, reveal a new one to me so that I may live my life knowing that for which I exist. Amen.

A Pilgrim's Journal

- When were you like Elijah—avoiding responsibility because you were afraid of what others would do or say?

- How would you answer, "What are you doing here?"

- How are you living out your discipleship today?

The Breakdown

T WAS A DUMB THING TO DO, CHARLIE realized, after kicking the tire of his disabled automobile for the second time. The pain that radiated up his leg after the first kick should have been warning enough. But no, he was so frustrated and angry that he wound up and gave the tire a second kick.

Charlie limped to the front of the car and stuck his head under the hood, trying to make sense out of the jumble of hoses and wires.

"Modern contraptions," he muttered as his fingers probed around the maze of automotive technology. "You pay a fortune for these darned things, and they still aren't reliable." He restrained the urge to give the tire another kick. He said to himself, There was a time I could repair my own car, but now I can't even find the dipstick.

It was then that he heard footsteps. He looked around the side of the car and saw a man walking toward him. He didn't remember passing anyone along the way. It had been a very deserted stretch of road.

It was difficult for Charlie to tell the stranger's age. He wasn't young, that was for sure. But he wasn't old. His well-trimmed beard was streaked with gray, and his skin was weathered from exposure to the sun, wind, and rain.

But he had an ageless quality about him. The backpack strapped to his shoulders looked very heavy, yet he walked with ease, as though he was totally oblivious to its weight.

"Hi," the stranger called out. "Having trouble?"

"No, I'm frying eggs on my engine," Charlie mumbled. Then, so that he could be heard, he spoke up, "Of course I'm having trouble. Why else would I be standing by the side of the road with my head stuck under the hood of my car? Whenever you see anyone like this, it's a sure bet that there's trouble.

"My, aren't you a bit testy? I was just trying to be neighborly. If you want me to get lost, just say the word and I'll continue on my way."

Now Charlie felt sorry for being so rude. "No, don't go. Please forgive me. It's just that I don't know what to do. Here I am, stranded in the middle of God knows where with a very expensive piece of junk that won't work."

"Mind if I have a look?" the stranger asked, unstrapping his sack and lowering it to the ground.

"Be my guest. Maybe you can make some sense out of the mess under there."

The newcomer stepped to the front of the car and surveyed the engine compartment. "Hmmm," he muttered as he stroked his beard. "Yep. Oh, yes. Ah, ha."

Charlie became excited as he listened to the man, and he watched carefully as the man took his inventory. "Do you think you know what's wrong?"

"Hardly," came the answer. "Actually, this is the first time I've looked beneath the hood of a car."

"What!" screamed Charlie. "Then what in the...?" Charlie checked himself. "Are you trying to tell me you don't know anything about cars?"

"That's right," the man said. "I've never owned a car in my life. In fact, I've never driven one either."

"Then why are you studying under the engine?"

"Oh, just curious. I've heard so much about them. I thought this would be as good a time as any to see one for myself."

"Great, just great. It's not bad enough being stranded, now I have to put up with…oh, never mind. Get out of the way, and let me see if I can find anything."

Charlie all but pushed the stranger aside and resumed his blind search for the problem.

"I think I know what's wrong," said a sheepish voice behind Charlie.

Charlie raised his head too quickly and banged it on the hood. "Ow! What are you talking about? You don't know the first thing about cars."

"Yes, but I do know that little wire there," he pointed to it, "looks like it ought to be connected to something— maybe that doodad just below it?"

Charlie looked. Sure enough, a tiny wire was dangling uselessly from its connector. "Naw, it can't be something as simple as that."

"Won't hurt to try."

"I guess not." Charlie connected the wire, got in the car, turned the ignition, and the car roared to life.

The stranger stood there with a wide grin on his face. Charlie looked appropriately humble. He got out of the car and went up to the stranger and offered his hand. "I guess I owe you an apology. The least I can do is offer to take you as far as I can."

"There's no apology needed, and it's mighty kind of you to do so."

The stranger started to lift his backpack into the car, but Charlie ran around him. "Here, let me get it for you."

"Don't bother. You won't be able to lift it."

"Nonsense," Charlie said as he grabbed the straps with both his hands. When he tried to lift it, he went down on his knees.

"I told you you wouldn't be able to lift it." The stranger took the straps from Charlie, who was still on his knees, and hefted the backpack with what seemed to be little effort. They got into the car and started down the road. "Where are you going?" Charlie asked.

"Wherever the road takes me," answered the stranger.

"Are you homeless?"

"I guess you might say that."

"Gee, that's too bad. How long have you been without a home?"

"Just about as long as I can remember."

"You're all alone then?"

"I am now. I used to travel around with some friends, but they're all gone now."

"It must be tough being lonely."

"I'm alone, but I didn't say anything about being lonely."

"Yeah, I guess you're right."

They rode in silence for a while. Then the stranger turned and said, "Look, Charlie, I think we have to talk."

The car swerved to the right as Charlie applied the brakes. The tires squealed in protest at the abrupt stop.

"You called me Charlie. How did you know my name? I never told you it. Who are you anyway?"

"It doesn't matter who I am. But what I have to say to you does. You're a great guy, Charlie, with a lovely wife and fine kids. You and they do not deserve what you are going to do to them and yourself."

"What do you mean?"

"Well, there's that little indiscretion with Millie at the office, for one thing."

"That's over."

"Yes, but only because Millie put a stop to it. And there is that shady deal you are on your way now to finalize."

"My business needs the money. Besides, who'll know? Everybody does it."

"You'll know, Charlie, and you are the one you must face every morning when you look in the mirror. It's not worth it. The other things you do that sap your dignity aren't worth it, either. It's beneath you. You're better than all that. Why, Charlie, you are my Father's child, created in his image, just a little less than the angels themselves. And what you are doing isn't worth it."

Charlie sat staring out the windshield, his hands tightly gripping the wheel. "I know," he whispered, "I know. I guess it took someone else to hold up the mirror so I could see what I am really like. But what can I do?"

"Let go of all of that. Become what God has made you. You can do it. Just walk away from that stuff. You'll be surprised how good things can be."

"You're right. I will. In fact, I'll begin by turning around and going home. To hell with the deal. I can make it without it."

"That's the way, Charlie. I know you can do it."

"But, if I turn around now, I'll have to leave you off."

"That's fine. This is as far as I am going, anyway. Just let me get my backpack."

He stepped out of the car, opened the back door and lifted the pack onto his shoulders. His knees buckled slightly under the weight.

"That's a mighty heavy backpack," Charlie observed. "I couldn't budge it."

"You can't carry what is in this pack. Only I can. In fact, talking with you has made it a little heavier."

"What's in it?"

"What's in my backpack? Sins, Charlie. I carry the sins of my brothers and sisters in my backpack."

He closed the door, and Charlie made a U-turn and drove away with a wave to the stranger.

Charlie watched him in his rearview mirror until he could see him no more.

Prayer

Lord, I confess that all too often I use "I'm just human" as an excuse. Help me to realize what that really means: that I am made in the image of the Creator, that I am God's child, and that my sins have been forgiven, and I am redeemed by grace. To be human cannot become an excuse for a sinful nature but an affirmation of who and whose I am. I am sorry for the burden of my sins that you had to carry. Amen.

A Pilgrim's Journal

- What does being redeemed (ransomed) by Christ really mean to you?

- You are created in the image of God. What does that mean?

- What sins are you carrying by yourself that need to be given up to God? Write a certificate of release and let them go.

The Pledge

ORE PEOPLE WERE MAKING USE OF THE little chapel at Community Hospital than had been expected. In fact, the local churches had to wage a fierce battle to convince the hospital's board of directors that funds spent on a chapel would be "cost effective." After many hearings and heated debates, the board relented and agreed to give partial support if the churches would raise the balance of the funds necessary for the project.

And now Community Hospital had a beautiful and well-appointed chapel for prayer and meditation. Those who planned it were sensitive to all expressions of faith and did their best to incorporate this in the design. The result was a place where people wrestled with their hopes and fears in serene silence. And the care of this place where people and God communed was Julio's pride and joy.

Ever since the chapel had opened its doors, Julio was responsible for its custodial care. He fastidiously vacuumed the plush carpeting the first thing in the morning and the last in the evening. The brass gleamed brilliantly as a result of his constant polishing. Julio always arranged the chairs in neat, straight rows and made sure the bibles and prayer books were placed in the racks in such a way that they invited people to use them.

Whenever someone came into the chapel, Julio would retreat into the shadows so as not to disturb his or her prayer. Usually, he would himself sit or kneel and pray to the Lord.

He would sometimes hear the prayers of others, uttered out loud. He did not intend to eavesdrop; he just could not avoid it. Some of these experiences had moved him deeply: the family that had thanked God for ending the suffering of their aged mother, the young man who prayed for the lives of his wife and unborn child, and the doctor who asked for the skill to perform a dangerous operation.

So, on this day, Julio sat in the back of the chapel, almost lost in the subdued lighting. The young woman who knelt at the front had distracted him from his own prayers. She was sobbing deeply as she twisted a small handkerchief in her hands. The muffled tones of the hospital paging system filtered through the chapel doors and broke the silence.

After a while, the woman raised her eyes and Julio heard her pray. "Oh, God," she pleaded, "please don't take Molly's life. Let her live and take mine instead." A new wave of sobs shook her shoulders.

A few moments passed, and she stood and turned away from the table that served as an altar. She noticed Julio sitting in the back of the chapel and gave a little, startled cry. "I didn't see you sitting there."

"Forgive me," Julio apologized, "I didn't mean to frighten you."

"Please, you didn't scare me," the woman said. "I just thought I was alone. I didn't expect to see you sitting there. I hope I didn't disturb you."

"Oh no, you didn't disturb me. My name is Julio. I take care of this chapel. Most of the time, when people are in this room, I simply sit back here and join them with my own prayers."

Julio noticed that tears had begun to well again in the young woman's eyes. She dabbed at the corners of her eyes and said, "I'm sorry, but I just can't keep from crying."

"Something is bothering you very much, isn't it?"

"Yes, it's. It's my daughter. She is very ill, and the doctors can't give us any guarantees. They're doing everything they can, but I feel so helpless. Molly is still so young; she has her whole life in front of her. It's just not fair."

"Yes, and that is when we feel that we would do almost anything to keep the worst from happening."

The woman nodded her head and lowered her eyes.

"I know what you are going through," said Julio. "It reminds me of my daughter Mar.. She was such a beautiful little girl and so full of life."

"Was?"

"Yes, we were living in the village where I was born. The nearest doctor and hospital were about a day's journey away. We were just too far for help. It was so hard on my wife. She never got over it. And I remember Marie many times, especially at night when I can't sleep."

"I'm sorry. I didn't know."

"Oh, you need not be concerned. In a way, memories of her keep her alive with us now. Besides, we have found strength through our prayers."

"I don't know if my prayers will do it. I've tried. But the fear is still there. I'd do anything to make sure that Molly makes it."

"Yes, even asking God to take your life instead of Molly's."

"You heard!"

"Couldn't help it. You'd be surprised how many times people pray that prayer."

"Did you?"

"That prayer? No, my request was different. I promised God I would serve him for the rest of my life if Marie lived."

"Well, you didn't have to follow through on it, did you? After all, Marie died."

"Oh, but I did. That is what I am doing now. It is my way of thanking the Lord for what I did receive."

"I don't understand. Your daughter died, didn't she?"

"Yes, but that is when I came to realize what I should really be praying for."

"What is that?"

"Well, for a faith that could help me overcome the grief we knew, for strength to continue on, for real hope in God's promise of life, for joy in being able to continue to serve Jesus and share his love with others. You see, I realize now that when I tried to make a bargain with God, God in turn opened a whole new life for me. That's why I am so happy to take care of this chapel where other people can discover God's love for them."

"But what if Molly…"

"Please trust God. We never want to lose those whom we love. But we do. Don't forget: Jesus was God's Son, and he was crucified. God knows. Believe me, God knows and understands. You will not go without comfort. And if Molly lives, you will have a good reason to rejoice in God's love."

Just then, the chapel door opened and a white-forced doctor looked in. "Ah, Mrs. Anderson, I thought I'd find you down here. Let's go up to Molly. She's been asking for you."

"You mean she's…"

"Yes, it looks as if she's turned the corner. Molly's still a sick little girl, but her chances look good right now."

The woman's tears started to flow freely again. "Thank you," she whispered to Julio as she hurried past him.

When the door closed, Julio was alone again. He turned toward the altar, smiled, and said, "Thank you." And he took a dust cloth from his back pocket and continued his loving service.

Prayer

When I bargain with you, Lord, it is usually to try to get my way, to have things work out the way I want them to. But I quickly learn that you will be done on earth just as it surely is in heaven. I need to tell you my concerns, and it is important to share my hopes and dreams. But, grant that having thus spoken I have the faith and courage to say, "Not what I will but what you will." Amen.

A Pilgrim's Journal

- What bargains have you tried to make with God? What did you learn from it?

- When did God's will turn you around so that you could see a whole new perspective?

- When were you ultimately led to place yourself in the hands of the Lord?

Liverwurst on Rye

RED STARED OUT THE LARGE PLATE GLASS
window that overlooked the empty parking
lot at Community Nursing Home, Inc. His
elbows rested on the Formica table where he
sat every day trying to remember where he
was and who all of these people around him were. Sights,
sounds, and smells foreign to his memory pushed and
tugged for recognition.

The sky was gray, and a strong breeze blew old dry
leaves and discarded candy wrappers across the hash-
marked macadam until they came to rest in a sheltered
corner where they would be gathered up and discarded. He
looked at his old, wrinkled, dry hands, hands that once
were strong but were now weak and almost useless.

His snow-white eyebrows knit together in a puzzled
look. There was something special about this day. The nice
girl in the white uniform told him, but he could not
remember. That was the way things were with Fred. His
old chums and family members and his experiences of long
ago were fresh in his mind. But today was a dense fog
through which he only momentarily saw when the fog
parted to give a glimpse of the present. The fog didn't
really bother him—most of the time. The pain of not

remembering came only when he knew that he did not know.

Just then a car pulled between two crisp white lines. A young woman got out of the car and reached in to retrieve her purse and another oddly shaped bag. When she turned toward the window, a faint spark cast some shadows of recognition in Fred's memory.

Fred lost sight of her as she walked toward the building and into the reception area. Soon she was forgotten.

Some activity across the room diverted Fred's attention away from the window. Some girls in white were pushing a woman in a Geri chair out of the room. One of the girls was saying something about the woman having her hair done and looking pretty for when some people will be visiting. The woman looked blankly at the one who was talking and smiled a toothless smile.

"Who are these people?" Fred wondered. "What are they doing here in my home?"

He turned his attention back to the window, noticing the red car for what he thought was the first time.

The scraping sound of a chair being pulled on the floor and the sound of someone clearing his or her throat made Fred turn back to the room. When he did, he saw a pretty young girl sitting across the table from him. She leaned forward and placed her hand on his.

"Hello, Gramps," she said softly, her lips smiling warmly.

The word "Gramps" struck a familiar note. He thought, "Some people used to call me 'Gramps.'"

"Do I know you?" he asked the girl.

"Yes, you do, Gramps. I'm Eileen. Your granddaughter."

"Oh, Eileen," he said still not fully remembering, "it is good to see you. Does your grandmother know you are here? Maybe we should call her. She will want to bring us some cookies and make some coffee."

Understanding, Eileen said, "No, Gramps, that's okay. Grandmother isn't here. She's not with us any more. I guess you do not remember when I came and took you to her funeral."

"Oh," Fred said, looking confused. He was sure he had just spoken with her a little while ago. Releasing that memory, he turned back to the girl. "What's it like outside today? I should go out and do the chores, but I can't seem to find my coat and shoes. It looks cold out there. Is it?"

"Yes, it is. It is cold and damp," she answered.

Fred's gaze became distant. He thought of having to fix the leak in the roof of the old house. "There's always so much work to do around here," he said, "I don't know if I'll have time to—"

"Gramps," Eileen said, calling him back to the present. "I brought you something. You said you were hungry for it the last time I was here."

"What is it?" he said excitedly, always liking surprises.

"Why don't you guess? I'll give you a hint. It is your favorite sandwich."

Fred's face became radiant. "Liverwurst?"

Eileen laughed and nodded "yes."

"Does it have a slice of onion?"

"A thick slice of a sweet, juicy, Bermuda onion," she told him, "with a lot of catsup."

"Oh, boy," Fred exclaimed, "do I like liverwurst sandwiches! Did you put it on rye bread?"

"The darkest rye I could find."

Eileen unwrapped the sandwich and gave half of it to her grandfather, who immediately started to eat it with gusto. She unfolded a napkin and placed it in front of him. She thought to herself how pleased she was to have checked at the nurse's station and received permission to bring this lunch to her grandfather. How she loved this old man. She had so many wonderful memories of her grandparents.

"My, that is good," he said eyeing the second half of the sandwich. "Do you know what would go well with this?" he asked.

"Yep," Eileen said as she reached down and into the bag that lay on the floor. When she withdrew her hand, she held a chilled can of Fred's favorite beer. Droplets of moisture ran down the side of the can. Eileen opened it and poured its contents into a plastic cup. Fred took a long deep drink and continued with the other half of the sandwich.

Eileen watched and thought, "Such a simple pleasure and yet it means so much. Gramps is enjoying himself. I have not seen him as happy as this for a long time. I've always wanted to do something special for him, but all I can do is bring in a sandwich once in a while. It's not that much at all."

Fred finished the last of his sandwich and drank the remaining beer in the cup. "Oh, that was good. Thank you." He looked at the young girl seated across the table from him. "Should I know you?" he asked.

"Yes, Gramps, you know me. I'm Eileen, your granddaughter. I must go now. I'll see you again in a couple of days. Is there anything you need?"

Being uncertain of what to answer he said, "No, I do not think so. If I need anything, grandmother will be able to go and get it."

Eileen stood. "Take care of yourself, Gramps."

"I will. Be careful. Button your coat because it looks cold out there. Come again."

Eileen turned to leave.

Fred said, "Oh, uh...uh...young woman. I am hungry for something."

Eileen laughed. "Yes, Gramps, I know. Liverwurst on rye."

Prayer

We live in an age of spectaculars and extravaganzas with glitter and glamour, and yet some of the most splendid moments are quite common and simple: a glass of cold water given to someone who is hot and thirsty, a kind word shared with another, or an embrace or a hand on the shoulder to express sincere oneness. These are the things that really matter, don't they, Lord? No act of love is so small that it is insignificant. Help me to be satisfied with smaller things. Amen.

A Pilgrim's Journal

- What small ordinary act of love did you perform that was received as a generous gift?

- What small thing can someone do for you right now that would be meaningful and appreciated?

- Write a prayer of thanksgiving for a small gift received.

Never the Same Again

S HE WAS A STRANGER. WHEN PEOPLE SAW her as she walked down the main thoroughfare of the village, they knew they had never seen her before. Little did they know that they would not forget her.

They had no way of knowing that on that warm spring afternoon the lives of a number of people in the village would never be the same again.

She was tall and strong, pretty but not stunningly beautiful, and walked with proud aristocratic grace. Her smile, a simple turning up at the corners of her lips, projected more mystery than mirth. Her eyes, clear and sparking bright, seemed to see much more than what they looked at. She was simply but tastefully dressed.

"Who is she?" whispered people to one another or to themselves as she proceeded with determination to the village square. Some left what they were doing and followed her, curious to see what would happen. The cobbler left his bench, and an unfinished shoe remained on it. A housewife set aside dough ready for the kneading. The blacksmith walked away from a horse half shod. Children, playing hide and seek, ran behind her leaving those who were most cleverly hidden.

When the woman and her following reached the square, she sat down on the lip of the fountain and waited.

The people looked at each other with puzzlement. They waited to see what she was going to do or say but she was silent. She just sat there and looked from person to person with her bright, sparking eyes and enigmatic smile.

After a while, the people started to move, restlessly shifting their weight from one foot to the other. "Why doesn't she say or do something?" they wondered. Then, slowly at first, but in time with increasing numbers they turned and walked away returning to things they had left in order to find out something about this woman who had just walked into their village. But they returned knowing little more than they had before.

When the crowd had dispersed, the mysterious woman stood and continued to walk through the village until she came to the outskirts where an old, abandoned home, in need of much repair, stood by the side of the road. She pushed open the door that swung on rusty hinges, which noisily complained as they reluctantly opened. There she spent her first night in the village.

Early the following morning, before most of the villagers stirred from the warm comfort of their beds, the woman awoke and prepared herself for what was before her. She found a bowl left in one of the cupboards; it was left behind because of the large crack in it. In early light of the dawn, she walked by the side of the road in search of berries which she would have for breakfast.

After a while, the bowl reasonably full, she returned to the old cottage. On the way she met a mother and her son. They were going to the neighboring village where the woman cleaned the homes of the wealthier people. She always took her son with her, not as much for companionship as to be able to watch over him.

The lad walked beside his mother, keeping up with her quick pace even though his left foot dragged uselessly behind him. His expert use of the crutch revealed many years of use. He seemed not to mind his impairment, and he and his mother joyfully chattered as they made their way along the road.

The boy shouted his greeting, "Morning ma'am."

The woman smiled at him as she approached but her eyes were filled with sorrow as she gazed upon the boy's foot. Without saying a word, she knelt before the boy and looked deeply into his eyes. After what seemed to be a long time, she took him into her arms, lifted her eyes heavenward and moved her lips in a whispered prayer.

After she finished, she slowly stood and reached out her hand.

Both the mother and the boy looked at her with fear for they knew what she wanted. Looking at his mother to see if there was approval, the boy saw a slight nod.

Holding onto his mother's skirt in order to keep his balance, he handed his crutch to the woman. Hesitantly at first but then with more courage, he placed his weight on his paralyzed foot, expecting at any moment to lose his balance and fall. But it did not happen. His foot was healed.

His mother, overcome with joy, hugged her son close to herself, forgetting the other woman for a moment. When she finally remembered, she turned to thank her, but she had already resumed her journey home. And as she walked, holding her bowl of berries, she dragged her left foot behind her in a painful limp.

That day the villagers noticed this strange transformation, and others that were to come. After restoring sight to the blind beggar, her own bright and sparkling eyes were shrouded in a gray mist. After skin sores disappeared from a young girl, the woman's clear complexion broke out in red blotches. Her neat and well-kept hair fell in disarray as she went from person to person touching, healing, freeing, liberating. At the day's end, an old, bent, pain-ridden, lame, and nearly blind woman was led by one of the villagers to the old abandoned cottage. Knowing that death was near, he remained and kept vigil. And late in the night, she took her last breath.

Her death was announced to those who had followed and waited outside. They did not understand. There was so much they didn't know. All they really knew was that she came among them and took upon herself that which held others in bondage.

Deciding to return early in the morning to tend to her burial, they all went home. But when they returned the following morning, she was not there.

In another village in another part of the kingdom, the day was just beginning. The people were stirring, and the business of the new day had begun.

She was a stranger. When the people saw her as she walked down the main thoroughfare of the village, they knew they had never seen her before. Little did they know that they would not forget her.

Prayer

You come to us, Lord, and you take upon yourself our human nature. On the cross you become the sin offering in our place. When I am confronted by your love, mercy, and grace, I cannot keep living my life with a "business as usual" attitude. I can never be the same once I have beheld your divine glory. At the mention of your name, I bend the knee and confess that you are the Christ, the son of the living God. Amen.

A Pilgrim's Journal

- In what ways has the presence of Christ changed your life?

- How would your life have been different if you did not know Jesus as Lord?

- When did the spirit of Christ pervade your life without your being aware of it?

A Sack Full of Love

NCE UPON A TIME, A PILGRIM FOUND herself deep in a dark and seemingly unending forest. Some of the folk in the village where the forest began called it the "Enchanted Forest." Others referred to it as the "Forest of Enlightenment." Whatever it was, the forest was vast and the traveler wondered if she would ever see the other side.

The day wore on and soon the shadows became long. Knowing that she would soon be plunged into darkness, she started to look for a place where she could spend the night as comfortably as one can in a forest. As she rounded a bend in the path, she saw, off to the side, almost hidden by trees and other vegetation, a small home. It was old and appeared to be severely beaten by the weather. Smoke was coming from the chimney, but there was no sign of anyone there. The house was dark and quiet.

The young woman followed a narrow path to the door of the home and rapped softly on the door. Not expecting to hear anything, she was startled when a weak voice called from inside, "Come in."

The door swung hesitantly on old, worn hinges. As she stepped inside and her eyes became accustomed to the dim light thrown into the room by a fire on the hearth, the young pilgrim saw an old woman sitting next to an older man who lay on a bed.

"My husband is sick," the crone said, "and I have injured myself so that I can barely take care of him. We have so little. Please take what you need. Spend the night if you wish. We will stay here and die together."

"You'll do nothing of the sort," responded the pilgrim firmly. "Here, let me see what is wrong." After examining the old woman carefully, she concluded that an arm and a few ribs were broken in a recent fall. She cleaned the abrasions on her legs and face and carefully set the broken arm. Tearing material into strips, she wrapped the woman's rib cage to give support until the ribs healed.

"There," the sojourner said after she had finished caring for the woman, "now let's see what is wrong with your husband." With deft and agile fingers, she probed here and there, listened to his heartbeat, and asked a few questions. "Have you any water" she asked the woman, "so that I can make a tea of some roots and herb I carry with me?"

The old woman went off as quickly as her feeble legs could carry her and soon returned with a cup full of clear, cold water from a well. The wayfarer reached into her backpack and withdrew packets containing the ingredients from which she made the medicinal tea. The old man protested at its bitter taste but was encouraged to drink it all.

Since night was falling, and there did not seem to be much food in the house, she again reached into her backpack and took out all of the food she carried and provided what was probably the most tasty and nutritious meal the elderly couple had in many days. After they all had eaten their fill, they all settled down for a peaceful night's sleep.

Instead of leaving the next day as was expected, the young woman stayed on and cared for the old couple, nursing them back to health. She hunted and trapped small game and filled the larder as well as replenished her own supply of food from which she fed them. She gathered roots, berries, herb and other foods found in the wild.

Many times the sun rose and set while the wayfarer cared for the couple who slowly regained their strength. The old man recovered from that which was sapping his strength and the bones of the old woman mended. Little chores and major ones around the house were done, and soon the old house was put back in order once again.

Finally, early one morning just as life started to stir once again in the forest the young woman announced that she was going to have to be going on her way. "I am a pilgrim on a quest that beckons me. You," she said turning to the old man, "keep drinking the herbal tea I made for you until it is all gone. Each day you will become stronger, and soon you will be doing everything you had been doing before." And turning to the woman, "And please be careful around that steep embankment. I don't want you falling again and hurting yourself. You both should be just fine now. But, when I return this way again, I will stop and look in on you and make sure all is well."

As they were saying their farewells, the two old people looked at one another. With bright shining eyes the husband gave a slight nod to his wife. She scurried over to the ancient bed in which he had been laying, reached underneath, and started to drag something out from under it. "We do not have much to give you," he said holding up his hand to stem the protest the young woman was about to make, "but my wife and I want you to have this sack."

An ordinary sack was placed at her feet. From the way it was carried, it had to be heavy. "You really do not have to give me anything, but I do thank you and will accept it only because I see that it means so much to you for me to have it. It looks so heavy. What is in it?"

The woman smiled. "Why, child, it is a sack full of love."

"Yes," added her husband, "but I feel that we must warn you. Be very careful that you do not run out of love. Always keep the sack full."

They said good-bye, and the sojourner continued on her way pondering the strange gift and the words of warning. "How does one keep a sack full of love full?"

Before midday she noticed that the trees were thinning and that she was starting to emerge from the Enchanted Forest of Enlightenment. Further down the road, she saw smoke that hovered above the roofs of the homes in the next town. Looking forward to meeting the people who lived there, she continued on her way.

The folk in the town were very friendly. She stayed a number of days and enjoyed hearing their stories and sharing the fare they offered her. And once again, she returned to her journey. When she picked up her backpack and the sack full of love, she noticed that the sack was somewhat lighter. "That's strange," she thought, "I didn't open the sack all the time I was here, and yet, it seems to have been emptied of some of its contents." This was a deep mystery to her.

She was no sooner out of town when she came upon a young boy who sat by the side of the road and was crying pitifully. "Why are you crying, child?" she asked.

"I'm lost and afraid. My mommy will be worried, and I'm scared I won't be able to get home."

"Come," the woman said, "let me dry those tears, and then you and I will go and see if we can find anyone who knows where you live." She wiped the boy's tears on a handkerchief she produced and make him blow his nose. "Now, let's see where you belong."

Together they returned to town, stopping people and asking them if they knew the child and where he lived. After almost a half a day of searching, they finally came upon someone who recognized the lad and informed the pilgrim that he lived way on the other side of town and out in the country. "It is a long distance from here," he added.

"It doesn't matter. I will see that he gets home safely."

As twilight was descending, they finally came to the lane that the boy recognized, and he started to run, calling his mother. The back door opened and a woman, a widow, ran down the lane and enfolded her son in loving arms.

The young woman was introduced to the boy's mother who invited her to sup with them and stay the night. She accepted the kind offer and was given a fine meal and a comfortable bed.

After breakfast the next day, she explained her mission and said that she had to continue on her way. The boy didn't want her to go, and his mother tried to assure her that it would be no bother if she stayed. The offer was kindly declined.

But then a strange thing happened. As she picked up the sack full of love, it seemed heavier. "Did they put something in my sack that I didn't see?" she wondered.

Well, she continued on her way until at last, after stopping many times to help those who needed it, she reached her goal, and the quest was accomplished. It was worth every ounce of strength it took for her to travel all that way.

The time came for her to return and, as promised, she traveled through the Enchanted Forest of Enlightenment, pausing along the way when she needed to do so. Finally, she entered the forest and came to the home of the elderly couple. When she knocked and opened the door, the reaction was one of absolute joy. They greeted one another with hugs and kisses, laughter and tears.

Both the husband and wife appeared to be in good health.

"I see that you still have the sack full of love," the old man observed, "and it seems to be full."

"Yes, I do still have it. It is not only full, but I do believe there is more in it than when you gave it to me."

The husband and wife looked at one another and chuckled.

"Tell me, child," the woman said, "has the Enchanted Forest of Enlightenment taught you anything?"

"Oh, yes," the returning pilgrim said. "When I left here, I was puzzled by your warning and was not sure how to keep the sack full of love from running out. I thought that if I kept it tied shut none could get out. But when I did that, the sack became emptier and emptier. It was then that I realized that the only way one keeps from running out of love is by giving away as much love as possible. The more I gave, the more I had. And now I have this sack full of love and, producing a second one, this one I am returning. Who knows? Maybe someday another pilgrim will be by this way who will be taught the lesson of the Forest of Enlightenment.

They talked long into the night. And when they finally went to sleep and the crescent moon hung in the middle of the sky, all of the creatures in the Enchanted Forest of Enlightenment gathered in the clearing and celebrated.

Prayer

The world I live in keeps telling me bigger is better and more is to be desired over less. But the more I have, the less remains, and the bigger things get, the more unreliable they become. You have given me the greatest gift there is: the gift of love. I must remember that love cannot be kept but must be given away in the same way a butterfly in captivity will die. And I certainly have enough for my life because, O Lord, your grace is sufficient for me. Help me to give your wonderful love as a gift to those who are not loved. Amen.

A Pilgrim's Journal

- In what way(s) have you discovered that the more love you give away, the more you have?

- Who has recently loved you in an unconditional and unselfish way?

- Read 1 Corinthians 13. What does this say to you in light of the story?

Reflections in the
Water

THE RAYS OF SUNLIGHT FILTERED THROUGH the stained glass windows, casting colored reflections on the water. A veil of silence hung draped over the congregation as a small group of people walked forward. One of them cradled a tiny baby and gazed lovingly into the child's eyes. By her side, a young man held her arm. Behind these three, an older couple walked straight and proud. Safely nestled in her mother's arms, the baby sought an elusive thumb.

Pastor Karlsonn stood at the baptismal font and waited as the small procession came forward. Years of dedicated service had etched their journey on his face, but the sparkle of his eyes and the creases at their corners gave evidence of a joy that radiated from within. The graying hair at his temples betrayed the hours he spent giving strength in times of weakness. His firm mouth, slightly turned up at the corners, testified to both his sensitivity and firm resolve.

How many times have I been here, he asked himself. How many children have I held in my arms as I said the words, "I baptize you"? He remembered how, over the years, his reverence for the mystery of baptism had changed. At first, that reverence had not quite reached the mystical peak he had reserved for the sacrament of the altar. Oh, baptism was a sacred moment, but it seemed to be missing something.

Then, something had happened. What was it? When was it? He was not even sure he could identify a specific moment or cause.

Regardless of what caused the change or when it happened, he now sensed the same awe and wonder when his cupped hand lifted the baptismal water as when he held the bread and wine of the Eucharist.

The movement of the colors in the water drew his attention. He looked and saw a reflection. It was not his own. In the water, he saw the face of Todd, his son, the oldest of this three children.

Memories of the day of Todd's baptism flooded his mind. As he held Todd in his arms, he became aware of the hopes and dreams this child represented. In a way, Todd was the extension of himself. Though he had no way of knowing what the years would bring, his son was the seed for the future. He felt again the joy and fear that filled his heart when he remembered that Todd was not only his child but God's, too.

The water's surface stirred, and the image changed. Todd's face was replaced by Maria's. He recalled that day Maria had walked into his office, battered and bruised. It took a while before she controlled her sobbing enough to speak. Her husband had just taken out his fury on her, as he often did. When he inquired why she stayed in the relationship, she had replied, "Oh, but he is a good man. I guess it is really my fault that he becomes so angry."

They met frequently, and he tried to counsel he as best as he could, but he was always afraid that it would be to no avail.

One day, Maria told him she had never been baptized and would like to receive the sacrament. That celebration was a joyful one. At that time, adult baptisms were few and far between. It was not long after that when his phone rang a little after midnight. It was the hospital. The emergency room nurses had found his name and phone number in Marie's purse. "She's dead," they told him. "The beating was too severe. We couldn't save her."

Marie's innocent face smiled sadly up at him from the water.

Child of God, he prayed silently, I hope you have found peace.

The surface of the water moved rapidly as reflection after reflection passed before his eyes. Most of the faces he recognized: people whom he had baptized or who had brought their children to him for the holy rite. Who are these people? he asked himself. Why are they appearing to me now?

As the waters stilled, one more reflection returned his gaze. It was his own. And, in that moment, he knew. All the faces reflected in the water were images of the people who made up his family in Christ. They were relatives and friends, strangers and acquaintances, the living and the dead—all his brothers and sisters reborn in the waters of baptism. They were his "cloud of witnesses"—the men, women, and children with whom he was united in the Lord. Then a nervous cough interrupted his reverie.

As his eyes cleared, he saw behind the colored patterns made by the light from the windows a whole new set of faces reflected in the water. He lifted his head and saw them standing before him, proud parents Julie and Dave and grandparents Henry and William. Little Danielle tried to focus on the thumb that continued to elude her.

Pastor Charleston looked at her. So tiny and innocent, she was the vessel of her parent's dreams. She was about to be born into a family of faith.

Dear God, he prayed in his heart, behold your daughter, their child, my sister. As he picked up the liturgy book, he saw one last reflection in the water.

It was the face of Christ.

Prayer

It was quite an event, but I do not remember it, Lord. Mom and Dad told me stories about that day. Even though my memory does not hold it, I know it was the most important day in my life. Often the fact that I am baptized fills me with sheer wonder and to know that you have received me as your child is a source of endless joy. Thank you, Lord. I pray that I can live faithfully as your child and that you can proudly claim, "Here is another one of my children." Amen.

A Pilgrim's Journal

- What is significant about your baptism?

- Knowing that you are God's child, what special expectations do you have?

- How can you make the anniversary of your baptism a more special day?

The Wait Is Over

HE COMMUNITY PARK IN THE CENTER OF town was usually buzzing with activity. Older folks would sit at small tables playing a game of checkers, chess, or pinochle. Others would sit on benches toasting in the warm rays of the sun while remembering the way things were and wondering why things are. From the play area squeals would be heard as children slid down the sliding board, teetered on the totters, and spun on the merry-go-round. Over by the swings, the timid would shout, "Not so high, mommy!" while others seemed to want to grasp the clouds in their hands. Young mothers pushed strollers along the paved paths while their infants cooed and gurgled with delight as kaleidoscopic shapes upon which they would be unable to focus pass before their eyes. Even the pigeons and squirrels would be a flurry flying or hopping from one person to another panhandling a few scraps of bread or the leftover popcorn from the previous night.

But, not this day. The park was deserted. The chessboards were empty save for the fallen kings lying on their sides awaiting the start of a new challenge and a new game. The sun's rays warmed vacant benches. The teeter-totters pointed at the clear azure sky while the swings stood at attention. No turning wheels of the strollers could be heard. All was quiet. Even the pigeons and squirrels abandoned their familiar haunt and could be seen or heard nowhere.

The park was empty—except for the one figure who sat on a bench near the general's statue. He was well known in town and would often come to the park to be with the others. But today he was alone. It was a strange sight. In fact, it was almost an eerie sight.

He sat in the middle of the bench and was flanked on the one side by a large pile of books and magazines and on the other with an oversized picnic basket and thermos of hot coffee. In his one hand, he held a book from which he read while he absently gnawed on a leg of chicken held in the other hand. Every now and again he would lift his eyes from the pages of the book and look in either direction as though he were waiting for something or someone. But seeing nothing or no one, he would return to the open pages of the book.

All was strangely quiet save for the occasional sounds and smells which the soft breeze carried his way from the edge of town: sounds of a calliope, the trumpeting of elephants, and the roar of big jungle cats, and the aromas of roasting peanuts, popping popcorn, pink cotton candy, and hot dogs on a grill.

All day long he sat on the bench, reading, eating, and watching.

Toward the late part of the afternoon, close to the time when the women of town would start preparing their evening meals, this solitary figure looked up and saw that someone was walking down the path. Well, to be accurate, he was better able to hear than see him. He was still pretty far away, too far to notice any characteristics except for the exceptionally large shoes the stranger wore that made a loud flapping noise as he walked.

As he drew near, more distinguishing characteristics could be seen. He was curious to say the least. His trousers were baggy and very large around the waist. The wide red and blue vertical stripes clashed with the plaid jacket that was so small it could not be closed. A brilliantly flowered necktie was worn over a green T-shirt with "Save The Children" emblazoned in large yellow block letters. A miniature Hamburg was perched smartly on the top of the stranger's bald head between tufts of fluffy orange hair. And his pure white face was most interesting with its star-shaped eyes, exaggerated smiling mouth, and round red nose. From the lapel of his jacket drooped a very large flower.

Flap, flap, flap. The noise of the very large shoes hitting the paved path grew louder as the strange apparition drew nearer until at last he came to where the lone inhabitant of the park sat between his books and picnic basket.

Their gazes locked as they wordlessly looked at one another for what seemed to be a long time. It was the newcomer who spoke first.

"Hi!"

"Good day," came the formal reply.

They lapsed into silence as they continued to stare at one another.

"What are you doing here sitting on the park bench?"

"Waiting."

"Waiting? Waiting for what? A train?"

"Hardly," the man said with a note of disdain. "I'm waiting for the circus."

"The circus?"

"Yes, the folks in town told me that the circus is coming so I decided to sit here and wait for it."

"But, pilgrim, don't you know. It's already here. Listen. Can't you hear it? There—that's the calliope played by Made the bearded lady. The big cats are roaring which means that they must be getting ready for their act. And you can't mistake the trumpeting of the elephants. Do you hear it?"

He nodded as he took another bite out of the chicken leg.

"And don't you smell it? The roasting peanuts, popcorn, cotton candy, and hot dogs? Breathe in deeply. Can't you smell the circus?"

He took a deep breath, thought for a moment, and cocked his head indicating that he did.

"You don't have to wait any longer, friend. The circus is here, just on the edge of town."

"Maybe so, but I think I'll just wait here. The people said that it is going to come, and maybe if I wait here long enough, I'll see it." He opened his book and went back to his reading, indicating that the conversation was over.

Flap, flap, flap. The huge shoes beat out their slow, sad cadence as the orange-hairdo stranger walked away, shaking his head and saying over and over, "But it's here now. The circus is here." He was so sad that even his painted on smile turned upside down.

And so it was that the man sat on the park bench and waited. The town folk brought books and magazines to replace those he had read. His picnic basket was replenished and the thermos filled. When it grew cold, they would come and cover him with blankets to ward off the chill.

And year after year the circus would come and put up the big top just on the edge of town. "The circus is coming," the man would be told. "Maybe this year I'll see the circus," he'd tell himself, checking his supplies and settling in one more time.

He would sit by himself in the community park on the bench closest to the general's statue. The soft breeze would carry the sounds of the calliope, trumpeting of the elephants, and roaring of the jungle cats. He would smell the roasting peanuts, popping corn, cotton candy, and hot dogs on the grill. Every year the circus came to town. The folks in town would come and tell him all about it. That's all he knew of the circus: what others said of it. And year after year he sat on the park bench and he waited to see it. But he never did.

Prayer

"The Kingdom is near," Jesus said. "The time is right; repent and believe." "Come and see—experience it for yourself," he is saying. But often I am satisfied with what others tell me about it. So much of my faith is secondhand. Lord, you stand at the door and knock. I want to open the door so that I can know you as Lord, savior, and friend. Amen.

A Pilgrim's Journal

- If the kingdom of God is where his will is done and his voice is heard, where has that kingdom recently broken into your life?

- Who has been that person who has brought you closer to experiencing the Word of God firsthand?

- What is Jesus saying to you when you hear, "The kingdom is close and the time is right—repent and believe"?

Going Home

A S THE FAMILIAR LANDMARK CAME INTO view, Jim wasn't sure this was such a good idea. After all, he had tried it once before, and the results were very depressing. It only goes to prove, he told himself, that they are right—you can't go home again.

Still fresh in his memory was the day when he realized that his mother could not longer stay by herself. And she knew it, too. It did not take much coaxing to have her agree that it was time to lock the door on the homestead for the last time and come and live with Betty and him. Her decline in health was obvious and too many miles separated them to provide the needed care.

But equally difficult was the decision to put the home up for sale. He had lived there since he was one year old. It wasn't only a home. It was a treasure chest of memories. The sounds of celebrations past still echoed off of the walls. Oh, the stories that the home could tell: stories about Christmas celebrations that defied description, stories about the pleasures and pain of growing up, stories of the joy of births and the sorrow of deaths.

And Jim's wife and children were a part of those memories as well. The realization that an era of life ended when the home was sold was as real for Betty, Jim's wife, and John, Beth, and Thomas as it was for himself. Whenever the family is together, which isn't very often these days, they would most assuredly lapse into reminiscing—recalling each room and the strangely mysterious quality that each it held.

But that is all gone now. The reality of how far removed he was from what used to be was the day he tried to go back. He drove past the home a couple of times, craning his neck as he drove, to take in each visible inch he could see. The last time he drove by the new owner stepped outside of the front door. Jim's heart beat madly. He stopped the car, got out, and went to the man. He introduced himself and explained who he was and how many years and wonderful memories were connected to the home. Jim did this with the silent prayer that he would be invited in to look around. But not only did the invitation not materialize, but the new owner did not want to talk.

So, Jim walked away, crestfallen, depressed, grieving. A very real part of him had just died. He had vowed that he would not do this again. The pain was too real and too deep.

That is why Jim was not sure that what he was doing was the right thing—because he was going back. This was a special occasion. John and Beth are both on their own now and Thomas, recently graduated from the university, was preparing to fulfill his requirements with the United States Navy. There will not be too many more times like this when parents and child or children can be together. When he told Tom and Betty that he would like to visit the cemetery, Tom, who had often said that he wanted to go back "to where Grandma lived," enthusiastically suggested that they make this a family experience.

The whole trip, which took better than an hour, was a rapid succession of memories as Tom recounted his early years and the experiences he had.

"Dad, do you think we'll have enough time to go out to camp?" Tom asked referring to the cabin where the extended family spent many summer weekends.

"We'll see," Jim answered, hoping to avoid any more unpleasantness than necessary. And, as if an omen was given, it started to rain.

After what seemed to be an eternity, Jim found himself on familiar turf. Tom asked to drive by the church they attended whenever they were visiting. As they did, Jim pointed out other landmarks: the library, city hall, the cemetery where some of the folks are buried, his old grade school. And then they were on the street that "took him home."

Things had changed, yet they were also comfortingly familiar. He stopped the car.

"They took down the fence, and look how big the trees that Dad planted have grown. Gee, the house looks nice. They are taking good care of it. I like the color of the siding they've put on. That sure beats having to paint the house. Boy, how I hated to have to paint the house."

Jim hadn't realized it, but he had been giving a nonstop narration and an excited one, too—talking about where the garden was, who the neighbors were, and what life was like growing up in this place. He resisted telling Tom how far he had to walk to school, and in the snow, too, because he knew what kind of a reaction that would get. He kept only one thought to himself. It seemed so small, smaller than what he remembered. Had his memory stretched or the land shrunk?

As they drove away, Jim was finally able to put a part of himself to rest. He had a good, warm feeling inside. But he was not entirely at ease. Tom wanted to drive out to the cabin. It wasn't far, maybe another twenty minutes, but was he up to it? Well, this was as much Tom's day as it was his own. Who knows when he would get the opportunity again. And as he grew older, Jim was aware of how much he wanted to avoid the "I wish I would have..." feelings that he often heard older folks talking about.

But seeing the cabin was a pleasant experience. A new person owned the land, and he kept it in fine condition. A few things were gone: the pavilion, flag pole, and small foot bridge. But enough remained to release the flood of memories that had been dammed up so long.

"Hi, there. Can I help you?"

Jim turned around. He had never seen the man before.

"I own this land. I saw you stop and walk around."

Jim apologized for intruding on his property and explained who he was. The stranger beamed a broad smile.

"Boy, am I glad to meet you. Maybe you can answer some questions for me. There are some things about what you had here that I don't understand."

And Jim explained how they used to pump water by hand from a spring across the creek, store water in a tank on the roof of the cabin to be heated by the sun, and a few other odds and ends.

When they finally said their good-byes, the owner said, "Come by again, any time you want to. You're welcome to come and have a picnic."

As they walked up the lane to the car, Tom said, pointing to the creek, "You know, Dad, this is where I caught my first fish."

The trip back to town was rather quiet. Jim, Betty, and Tom were all bathing in their own thoughts, both cleansing and purifying memories of the past.

One more stop: the cemetery. There Jim stood in silence. Mom and Dad rested side by side. He never made a big thing about going the grave site or putting flowers on the grave. But today was special. Today a part of Jim was born anew. A burden he had silently and privately carried had been lifted, and it felt good to come home once again.

As Jim turned to return to the car for the final trip to the place his children will visit and recall the memories of "home," he found Tom standing right behind him. Before he could say anything, Tom wrapped his arms around him. "Thanks, Dad! Thank you for a wonderful day. You don't know how important it was for me to come. Thank you very much."

Betty walked over to them. Jim put his one arm around his wife and the other around his son. Through a mist of tears he silently said, "And thank you for being here with me."

As they walked away, Jim knew that he didn't have to go home again.

Prayer

It is so hard to let go. Children move away, strange people live in places filled with our memories, and family and friends die. There is only one constant, and that is your love for us. Lord, you have promised that you go ahead of us to prepare that place where we will be united with you. When the time comes, grant that I will open my hands and release what I held dear in order to embrace that home that awaits me. Amen.

A Pilgrim's Journal

- What fond memories do you have of "home"?

- What recent moments did you share with another (or others) that opened the flood gates of memories?

- Take a trip back into your childhood and recall one of your most pleasant memories.

A Morning Cup of Coffee

BRUCE'S RECURRING DREAM WAS interrupted by the mind-jarring buzz of the alarm—and not a moment too soon. It was about to happen again, just the way it happened every other time. The situation never changes. He is about to address a large crowd of people when the embarrassment takes place. That is the only variable. He may have forgotten his notes, or he may not be at the right place, or—the ultimate embarrassment of all public speakers—he may not be wearing any pants.

But not this morning. The alarm, as harsh as it is, saved him from having to deal with another faux pas.

Nancy stirred beside him and hunkered down lower into the warm cocoon of the blankets, knowing that she still had some time to sleep.

Bruce will call her, and then she will have to start to get ready for another day of dealing with a room full of fifth-grade children. When speaking about her work, she would often say the word "children" with tone that would suggest that these beings were not of this world. For now she could surrender to a few more minutes of sleep while Bruce went through his ritual of waking up enough to face another day.

Bruce's unsteady hand reached out and fumbled for the button on top of the clock that would silence the incessant alarm. He had often thought of using a heavy mallet to end its noise once and for all. This particular morning the thought once again tried to surface in his foggy mind, but instead he found the button and peace and quiet were restored for one more day.

He had a routine which he flawlessly followed—not because he was a creature of habit but because that was the only way he could get started. It was simple, or so it would seem: a cup or two of steaming coffee, the morning newspaper, and a slow entry into the world that was in the process of waking up. But, without that first cup or two of coffee, Bruce was unable to cope with the day, people, or events until about noon.

With some effort, "I've really got to start my diet one of these days," he thought to himself, he swung his legs out from under the covers. His feet slid effortlessly into his slippers. He stood slowly, like an overweight newborn calf cautiously trying its legs for the first time. Determining that it was safe enough to remain standing, and after running his fingers through his tousled dark hair and scratching himself in places that itched, he started to make his way to the kitchen.

Bruce navigated the hallways of his home as if he were on automatic pilot. He carefully, but barely, missed the obstacles that were put in his way the night before when their children abandoned their toys before the cleansing ritual known as "the bath." After watching him one morning, Nancy could not understand how he avoided stepping on a toy, stubbing his toe on a piece of furniture, or falling over the family dog. He amazed her with his deft agility.

Without incident Bruce entered the kitchen, stopped, and breathed in deeply the enticing aroma of the brewed pot of coffee that awaited on the countertop. "Thank God for technology," he muttered, referring to the coffee brewer that automatically turns itself on before Bruce's entry into the new day began. "And thank God for a wife who remembers to get it ready the night before."

He shuffled across the tile floor and opened the cupboard above the coffee maker to retrieve a mug from the bottom shelf. Over the years, they had accumulated an impressive collection of mugs that were stacked five deep and three high. But at this time in the morning Bruce was not very selective, taking out the one his hand touched first.

He was about to reach for the pot of coffee when he noticed the mug in his hand. His brow creased questioningly. "That's strange. I don't remember using this cup before." What made it so unusual was its plainness. It didn't have a logo or illustration on it, not even a catchy proverb. It was just a plain white ceramic mug with a very thin green line that circled the mug just below the lip. He made a mental note to ask Nancy where or when they got this mug. But for now it would serve its purpose.

The rich, dark brown liquid splashed into the cup, sending up a tantalizing scent that caused Bruce's taste buds to kick into overdrive. He carried the cup to the refrigerator where he got a carton of milk.

What happened caught Bruce so off guard that he almost dropped the mug. Faintly at first, but increasingly with more brilliance, bright red gothic letters started to appear. With uncertain steps, he carried the cup and carton of milk and placed them on the kitchen table. He sat down heavily and stared at the strange mug as though it were an apparition.

Bruce looked closely at the message: "Like an unopened gift, this day awaits to reveal its treasure."

"Nice thought but not very realistic," Bruce said, thinking about how uneventful his life really was. It was the same old routine, day after day, and one day seemed to bleed into the next so that it was difficult to tell one from the other. "My days don't contain treasures. Landfill would be more like it."

As he was adding milk to his coffee, still puzzling over the cryptic message and how it got there, he heard the thump of the newspaper as it was tossed onto the front porch. He rose from the table and retrieved the paper, scanning the headlines as he walked from the front door, through the living room, and back into the kitchen. After he sat again at the table, he reached for his mug of coffee while starting to read the text under the headline: Riot Breaks Out—Three Killed, Scores Injured. When he brought the mug to his lips, his eyes were drawn away from the newspaper, like iron filings are attracted to a magnet.

"What happened?" He turned his cup from side to side. The message was gone. No sign of the red letters remained. "That is really curious. I wonder if Nancy knows anything about this."

Finally, he took a long drink of coffee. "AHD," he sighed, "it doesn't get much better than this."

His attention was then given to the newspaper. Article after article grated against Bruce's sense of right and justice. He read about fraud and incest, muggings and protests, accidents and disasters, graft and greed. Even the humor on the comic pages seemed to speak to the dark side of life.

"I don't know why I do this every morning. It is so depressing."

That's when it started to happen again, only this time the letters were bright orange and the gothic font was now a modern computer block. After a few seconds he read, "Hey Bruce, this day was made for you. Enjoy it!"

"Oh, no. Now I think I'm losing it. A different message and my name? No! It's not possible."

It was then that Nancy entered the kitchen. "Why didn't you call me? If I hadn't heard the children stirring, I would have overslept. You've never forgotten to call me before."

"Sorry. I didn't realize how late it was getting. It was this mug...."

"That mug made you forget to call me?"

"Wait! Let me explain. Messages keep appearing on it, different messages in different colors and styles."

"What? Are you feeling okay?"

"I feel fine. Here. See for yourself."

Nancy took the mug and turned it around. "I don't see anything. What in the world are you talking about?"

Bruce realized that the orange letters had vanished as mysteriously as they had appeared. "I swear, Nancy, there was a message on that mug. It even knew my name."

"Ugh, huh, I see. Honey, don't you think you ought to stop snacking before you go to bed? It puts you so out of sorts. Now, why don't you drink your coffee and get ready. You don't want to be late for work."

Well, that's what Bruce did, but his mind was occupied with the strange happenings. Halfway through his shower, he decided he was going to take this mug with him to work. If it did it again, maybe someone else would be able to see it and explain what the phenomenon was.

It was an unusual day. Harry, the driver for the week, noticed that Bruce was unusually quiet. He just sat and stared at the coffee mug he held in his hands. He wanted to ask Bruce what was going on but seeing how deeply Bruce was concentrating, he decided to wait for a more opportune moment.

And messages did appear on the mug and usually in connection with a related event, each time in different colors and print styles. Mid morning Charlie came into his office. He didn't like Charlie. Charlie was on his way up the corporate ladder, and he didn't care how he got to the next rung. Many people whom he had used and abused to get where he was were awash in the wake of his upward movement. And he even bragged about it. That's why he came in to see Bruce: to tell him about his latest conquest. After Charlie left, the mug produced forest green letters in a Roman font. The message was, "The little guy wins!"

After lunch Carol, the newest person to be hired, knocked on Bruce's door. He was up to his eyebrows in work and deadlines were quickly approaching. But when Carol asked if he would explain some things about her job that were giving her trouble, he put it all aside and gave her his undivided attention. After she left, he wanted to kick himself for giving her so much time. Now he surely would have to take some of the work home with him. Bruce then noticed the baby blue script on his mug that read, "He who serves leads."

That's the way it went all day. By the time he was ready for his commute home, Bruce had an impressive collection of proverbs and slogans that just popped up on his mug. One time there was even a graphic. That was when Bruce's boss, a regular pain, stuck his head into Bruce's office to make some inane comment about a project Bruce had just finished. That was when the "smelly face" appeared. But this one was different. The eyes were crossed and a tongue stuck out of the side of its mouth at an idiotic angle. The caption made Bruce laugh hysterically: Don't you just love it when genius pays a visit?

All the way home that evening, Bruce weighed the advantages and disadvantages of mentioning the mug and what happened to the rest of the family. A benefit would be the possibility of finding out where it came from and a possible solution to the mystery. On the minus side would be the possible suggestion that he ought to commit himself to a mental hospital.

Dinner in Bruce's household was always busy. Nancy usually tried to orchestrate some semblance of order and decorum while Jeff, Katy, and Ryan did their best to see that neither took place. Bruce was the ineffectual mediator, and Rusty, the all breed dog, sprinted from one to the other, catching dropped morsels of food before they even reached the floor.

"Hey Dad, where did you find my mug?"

Bruce nearly choked on the mouthful of mashed potatoes he was in the process of eating. It was Jeff who asked the question.

"Your mug?"

"Yeah, I just got it the other day. Isn't it neat? Did you see the way those 'Star Trek' figures appear and disappear when the temperature changes? It's just like when they're being 'beamed' by the transported room."

Bruce was flabbergasted. He didn't know what to say. He didn't see any images of people from the TV program. But, sure as God made little green apples, he did see some things.

"Yes," he stammered, "Yes, it sure is amazing. I wonder how they do it."

He didn't say much during the rest of the meal. He just couldn't let go of what had taken place that day. He remembered all of the proverbs and sayings and how they showed up right after something eventful had taken place. He though about how correct the first ones were earlier that morning. His day, that was not at all unlike any other day, was like a gift. Even though it was mundane, he found blessings and treasures. And it was his day, and he did enjoy it.

"But, I still don't know how it happens," he said just loud enough so that Nancy could not hear him over the noise of the children and the clanking of the dishes that were being stacked in the dishwasher. "I sure would like to know how...."

Bright purple script started to appear on the mug that was filled with steaming coffee. When Bruce read it, he smiled. At last, he understood. It read, "Lo, I tell you a mystery—not explain it!"

Prayer

You speak to your people through simple things, Lord. In fact, you were present to those whom you love in a common carpenter from the "nowhere" town of Nazareth. But today I do not trust those simple things. Like Elijah of old, I want to hear your voice in earthquakes, wind, and fire. I wait until I see your hand inscribing your message on a wall. But I must learn that you still whisper. I must lean forward to hear. You still come in simple things like the wonder of a snowflake or the love of a child, and, most amazing of all, you seek to come to others through the likes of me. It is a mystery. Amen.

A Pilgrim's Journal

- How has God come to you or spoken to you recently?

- In what way(s) has God been using you to as a presence to his people?

- When have you been most aware that God is near to you?

The King Is Dead:
Long Live the King

HE KING IS DEAD."
Word of the king's death spread throughout
the realm like a prairie fire fanned by hot
westerly winds. And the news was met with
predictability. Those who love him mourned;
those who feared him rejoiced; those who were jealous of
him coveted his throne; and those who were indifferent
didn't care.

The king was dead, and on the day of the funeral, his
loyal subjects gathered outside the walls of his palace. But
no one witnessed the funeral. By request of the king, the
only people to be present during the final hours after the
news was announced were his dear friend and special
counsel—the wise and honest Grand Vizier—and a beggar
from the streets of the capital whom the Vizier was to
select.

The crowd that waited was silent. The heaviness of
their sad hearts was communicated by the depth of sorrow
seen in their eyes. Only a soft murmur indicated that some
people were whispering.

Late in the afternoon, when the sun began its slow
decline in the west, the front doors of the palace opened
and through them walked the pitiful sight of the beggar
who was chosen to be a witness. A brief surge of the crowd

pressed forward to receive word of the king's final rest. But the forward movement ceased when the people saw the beggar dressed in torn and patched dirty clothes, wearing the signs of an untouchable.

The crowd parted and formed an aisle along which the beggar passed. His progress was slow as he leaned upon a crutch to bear the weight of his diseased body. And as he passed, all of the people turned away for fear that a look from his evil eye would pass his horrible disease on to them.

A figure appeared on the balcony of the palace. It was the Grand Vizier. For the first time that day, the noise in the crowd rose so that the Vizier had to hold up his hands to silence them.

"People of the realm and loyal citizens," he said addressing the crowd. "It is a sad moment that brings us together and all but one of the king's desires have been fulfilled. As you know, there is no heir to the throne."

"I am too old to be king, and the final desire of the king to be carried out is the selection of his heir. Starting tomorrow any person in the realm may appear in the court of the palace. There they may present to the king's advisors who they think should be king and why. After listening to everyone, the advisors will decide who shall be our king."

This was received with a mixed reaction. "Some of the advisors were not the king's friends," some protested. "A faction tried to overthrow the king," others remembered. "They will not have the welfare of the realm as their main concern," a few observed.

"Please, people of the land," the Vizier concluded, "please be patient. It is your king's wish. Let us pray that the advisors will choose wisely. Go home and pray. And come to help call forth our next king."

Early the next day the line to the palace court was long as many stood in the hot sun waiting for their chance to present their cause to the king's advisors.

The first in line was the general of the army. He was splendidly dressed in his uniform of chain mail and armor. The hilt of the broad sword which hung at his side glittered with the precious stones that were encrusted on it.

"I stand before you to proclaim that I should be king," he said with a loud and commanding voice. "I have fought and won many battles. Although I did not always agree with the king, I was loyal. It was only when he refused to go against the kingdom to the west did I seek to overthrow him. The king proclaimed this faith in me when he kept me in this place of authority. What more evidence do you need to know that I am the one he wanted to succeed him? If he didn't, I would no longer be in command of the army."

A few of the advisors stood and applauded the general. But others, not trusting him because of his previous behavior just sat and silently shook their heads.

The general was followed by the keeper of the treasury. His rich robes flowed as he strode into place. "I should be king," he said. "It is I who held this realm together. The king knew nothing of financial matters and gave me full rein to take care of them. To reward me, he allowed me to keep some of the wealth gleaned from the taxes and tribute paid by the people." He looked admiringly at the clothing he wore, evidently pleased with his wealth and stature.

"The next king," he went on, "will need to possess knowledge of business and treasury management. Surely you can see that I am the most qualified. Being appointed to my position by the king should be all the evidence you need."

Again, some among the advisors stood and applauded. They were the ones who received money for favors rendered to and on behalf of the court treasurer. But those who knew that the treasurer, in order to maintain his rich lifestyle, levied taxes far too heavy upon the people, and the fact that he was not known to turn away from bribes, did not respond.

On and on the parade of people presented themselves before the advisors. There were merchants who plied their trade along the caravan routes, military people who spoke of wars and strength, ordinary people who had visions of living in the palace, even a few of the insane who thought that they were king anyway. Day after weary day, people presented themselves until the advisors thought they could not stand to hear another request to be king. And, most certainly, a few of the advisors had their opportunity to present their own cases.

Finally, the line grew shorter and shorter until the last person in the queue stood before the advisors. He was a simple man, nervously twisting his hat in his hands. He dared not raise his eyes to the raised platform on which the advisors assembled.

The advisors laughed when they saw the peasant. One of them said, "Well, what do we have here? The cream of the ghetto? Speak up, man. Tell us your story so that we can get on with making our decision." Turning to the others, he said, "This should provide us with some sorely needed entertainment." And turning back to the nervous creature, he shouted, "On with it, man, why should you be king?"

With a voice just above a whisper, he said, "Oh, it is not I who should be king. There is another. I met him just a few day's ago, right after the king's funeral. He is a kind man. One night he gave the only food he had to a woman whose child was starving. He is a patient man. He never responds to those who scorn him. He is a strong man for he has endured more than any of us put together. He is...."

"Enough," the spokesman for the advisors interrupted. "Just tell us who this man is. Let us see him. Let him tells us about himself. Where is he?"

"Over there," the peasant said, pointing to the crowd that had assembled on the side of the court.

Out from the crowd hobbled the beggar. A gasp arose from the people. Some recoiled with revulsion.

Laboriously, the beggar hobbled with his crutch to the center of the court. The advisor's face was red with anger. "What are you doing?" he shouted. "This is no circus. Why should that wretch of a man be king?"

At that the beggar stood, threw off his ragged cloak and dropped his crutch.

"Because I am the king," came the answer.

There stood the king before his surprised and frightened court. "No, I am not dead. The Grand Vizier and I agreed that the only way for me to find the heir to my throne is to live among you and find him myself. I have found him, and he is that poor fellow you ridiculed so shamelessly. Everyone else sought the throne for himself. Money, power, greed, and prestige fueled this orgy of covetousness. He sought the qualities of a king in others. This man who stands before you shall be the next king. And woe to you who thought that your misdeed will be overlooked. There is a new day dawning in this kingdom."

Prayer

My Lord, what a strange kingdom you have. Strangers in the street are invited to the banquet, the least important are given places of honor, ninety-nine are left on their own while you go looking for the one who is lost, the diseased are whole and the influential ones are sick, common folk are disciples and religious leaders are clowns. Sometimes I don't understand it. Most of all, I find it hard to understand a king who dies but lives again. It is a mystery. But that is just fine, I guess, because life that is well seasoned with mystery is most exciting. Amen.

A Pilgrim's Journal

- What are some of the mysteries of faith you wonder about?

- Can you imagine yourself as one of the "chosen?" Why or why not?

- Think of a person who leads effectively through his or her humility.

The Express Line

HAT'S IT! NO MORE NICE GUY! I'M SICK AND tired of following the rules and having someone who doesn't do that get ahead of me."

The young girl at the checkout counter paused as she passed a package of pork chops over the scanner. Her eyes grew wide as she looked at Dan, who was pacing back and forth, swinging his hand-held basket like a pendulum. She looked at the woman at the next register with a "What am I supposed to do?" look in her eyes. It was answered with a puzzled shrug of the shoulders.

People with carts who had been standing behind Dan backed away and made their way to other lines carefully avoiding eye contact with Dan. A few heads came together and whispered comments questioned the sanity of the one who was showing growing agitation.

"Young lady!" Dan said with a commanding voice, "Young lady, I want you to call the manager. Get him here immediately before I do something irrational."

Obediently, she picked up her intercom phone, pressed the button, and said, her voice quivering noticeably, "Mr. Johnson to checkout three, please—and hurry!"

"Don't touch those bagels," Dan shouted, pointing to the package the girl was about to scan. She dropped them and moved back, putting as much distance as possible between herself and this strange man.

A young man in his middle to late thirties approached the line. "What is it, Linda?" he asked. "Your voice sounded as though there was an emergency."

Linda nodded and pointed with her eyes at Dan who swung around to face the manager of the store.

"I'll tell you what's wrong. It's her." Dan pointed to the little gray-haired woman in front of him.

"Excuse me, I don't understand," Mr. Johnson responded.

"No, you wouldn't understand, would you? It's people like you who are the cause of all the problems. You make the rules, but you won't enforce them. Then folks like myself end up getting the short end because we do follow the rules."

Mr. Johnson sighed. "I'm sorry. I still do not know what you are talking about. Maybe if you just calm down we can take care of what is bothering you."

"Don't tell me to calm down," Dan fumed. "I have a right to be upset. Just look at her order. Fifteen items. Count them. Fifteen! And the sign plainly states, 'Twelve Items Or Less.' Now, what are you going to do about it?"

"Please, Mr., er..."

"Godfrey. Dan Godfrey."

"Thank you. Mr. Godfrey, can we talk sensibly? You are making people around you uncomfortable."

"Uncomfortable," he almost screamed, "I'm talking about inconvenience, and you're worried about their comfort. Look, I've been coming to this store ever since it opened. I'm a good customer. You've never had a complaint from me before. But, it happens every time. I get just a few things, always less than twelve items. Then when I get in line, the person in front of me always has more. This is an express line. You have established the limits and posted them. Why should I have to wait just because some people can't count?" His last few words were said with a turn of his head toward the woman who was the target of his ire. She raised her head and turned away with a "humph".

"But, Mr. God, it's no big deal, is it?"

"Of course, it is. If fifteen items are acceptable, then the sign ought to say 'fifteen.' It doesn't. It says twelve. I just want what I deserve."

"Oh, I don't think you really mean that, do you, Mr. Godfrey?"

"You bet I do. It is time that those of us who live by the rules stand up and demand what we have coming to us."

"Are you sure that is what you really want? You do want me to enforce the twelve item limit literally?"

"Finally. That is what I have been saying all along."

"Well, if that's what you really want, I am going to have to ask you to move to another line, one that is not an express line."

"What? Are you mad? I can't believe this."

"Mr. God, you want me to limit items in the express line to twelve. You have more than twelve."

"I do not! Count them. There are eight."

"I find more, many more. For example, you have four oranges. Those oranges are sold individually. So, technically, you have four items there. Then there are the dozen eggs. It is true we do not sell the eggs one at a time, but you can purchase a half a dozen carton. That makes six more items. The chicken breasts are wrapped separately. You probably buy them that way for convenience. Nonetheless, I count four more items there. So far my total is fourteen, and you still have five more things in your basket which, if we were to enforce the restriction literally, can be counted as separate items. So, all in all you have more than twelve. Yes, even more than fifteen. I'm sorry,

Mr. Godfrey, you are in the wrong line. Now, do you still want to make an issue of this?"

Dan sagged like a sailboat that lost the wind. He was confused. He was still angry and indignant, and he did feel that he was right, but Mr. Johnson presented a very good argument. "Maybe being literal isn't the answer," he mumbled. "But, it's just that…oh, what's the use? I'm sorry."

He went to move to another line. Mr. Johnson caught him by the arm and said, with a wink, "If you don't make me kick that little old lady out of the line, I'll let you stay, too."

Dan flashed a sheepish grin. "Okay. And thanks."

It wasn't long before Dan was checked through and was on his way.

Mr. Johnson was helping the woman to her car with her groceries.

"That was one strange man," she said to him.

"He sure was, Mom. He sure was."

Prayer

Lord, I thank you that we do not get what we deserve—that your sense of what is right and just differs so much from our own. Without your grace I would surely be a lost sinner with no hope of being redeemed. The next time I look at the sins in the life of someone else remind me that I need first to look at the sins in my own life. When I hear your patient and gracious words of forgiveness, I can do nothing other than be forgiving. Amen.

A Pilgrim's Journal

- Think of when you judged someone else. What was the unfairness of it?

- God does not give us what we deserve. What does this mean to you, and what special message is there for you?

- God's grace is a gift freely given. Are you able to accept gifts graciously? What should be our response to the gift of grace?

Nothing in Return

NE DAY A LONG TIME AGO, LONGER THAN most folks can remember, a woman came to town. No one had ever seen her before. She roused curiosity among the people in town. There was just something different about her. Most of the time people shy away from people who are strange, but there was a sort of magnetism that attracted the town's residents to her.

From almost the very moment she arrived, she went about doing things in her unique way. The first person she met was an old widow who was on her way out of town to gather sticks for her fire so that she could cook and keep warm.

"Hello there, mother," the stranger hailed. "Where are you going on such a fine day as this?"

"I'm on my way to gather wood. I am all alone—no sons, husband, or daughters to help me."

"And why must you gather wood?"

"So that I may live. I make a meager living by selling the bread I bake and stews I mix. I also need the wood so that I can cook for myself and keep warm on the cold nights. It is hard work for an old lady. But I will die if I do not do it."

"Ah, well then, dear mother, let me come with you and help you for I am younger and stronger."

"Oh, thank you so very much," the old widow responded with sincere gratitude, "but do not bother because I will not able to repay you."

"I ask for nothing in return other than the joy of being able to share your burden."

The old woman continued to protest but the stranger paid no attention to her. So they both went into the forest.

Later, as the sun was beginning to set, the two women returned to town. A large bundle of sticks weighed heavily upon the shoulders of the stranger. Slowly, and with a little difficulty, they made their way through the streets and alleyways until they came to the widow's small home.

After she lowered the wood to the ground, the younger woman straightened, placed her hands on the small of her back, and stretched to relax her cramped muscles.

The widow said, "Let me at least repay you by making you a hot meal."

"Sweet mother, I do not want you to repay me. I have done this for you. It is a gift."

Shaking her head as she walked away, the old woman said, "I don't understand it. Thank you."

The stranger watched as the old woman walked away. Tears of sadness welled up in the corners of her eyes.

The next morning, a group of mothers and their young children were gathered in the center square. Their conversation was animated. Some were angry, others were disappointed, and the rest were bewildered.

Through the small crowd of women and children walked the stranger. "What is the matter?" she asked.

One woman, apparently the self-appointed spokesperson for the rest, answered, "We have a problem. Everyday we go out to the fields to work. It is important work because our husbands do not earn much money and what we earn helps us to keep food on the table and our children clothed. But one of us must remain behind to watch the children. We take turns doing this. The one whose turn it was today is ill and unable to watch the children. No one is willing to remain behind today because our need for money is too great."

"Do not fret anymore," the stranger said as she smiled at a little girl who was peeking out from behind her mother's dress. "I will gladly watch your children for you as you go to the fields to work."

"Oh, thank you so much," another mother said. She looked so young, almost too young to have given birth yet three small faces beamed up at her as she spoke. "Your offer is so kind but we cannot accept because we will not be able to repay you."

"I do not want you to repay me," the stranger stated. "I want to watch your children so that you can help to provide for them. It is a gift. Go on now, all of you. Off to the field with you. I will take good care of your children."

At first they were reluctant to leave their children with someone they did not know. However, when the mothers saw how quickly their children responded to the woman and how they were laughing and playing together, they left for the fields confident that the children would indeed be well cared for.

All day long the woman cared for the children. They played games and sang songs. In the afternoon, they sat on a hillside and the children listened with intense rapture as the woman told stories—stories that made them laugh and stories that excited their imaginations.

All too quickly the sun began to set behind the western hills. The women returned from the fields and gathered their children. "Oh, mommy," the children shouted, "we had so much fun." They told their mothers about their games and songs and the stories that the woman told.

The spokesperson from the morning once again faced the stranger. "We are indebted to you for caring for our children. On the way home, we were talking among ourselves and decided that we all would share some of what we harvested with you as a repayment for your kind act."

"Please do not give me your food in return for my gift. It is not payment that I seek. Please accept what I did with the intent with which is was offered."

Each one of the women thanked her as they herded their offspring together to make their way home.

As the last mother walked out of sight, the strange woman looked on, and tears of sadness welled in the corners of her eyes.

Day after day, the woman met someone in town who was in need of help in one way or another, and she gave the gift of herself. She carried mortar for a man whose helper was called away. He had to build a chimney before winter set in. It was very hard work. Though the chimney builder was unable to give her money, he did offer to pay her with a place to sleep and a good meal prepared by his wife yet she refused payment. Another time she milked a herd of cows so that the farmer and his wife could go to the church social. They brought some of the leftover food home to pay her for freeing them from their duties, allowing them to enjoy a night of fellowship yet she would not accept the payment. And each time, as she looked on, tears of sadness would well in her eyes.

One day, just a few weeks after she first came to town, she was holding a horse for the blacksmith as he nailed a shoe to the horse's hoof. Just when the smithy struck the last blow, the woman fell to the ground in a faint. He lifted her in his strong arms and carried her to the office of the town physician. News spread quickly, and soon everyone to whom she had given a gift of herself gathered outside the doctor's house.

At about noon, the doctor came out and stood on the top step of his porch. He shook his head. "She's no longer with us," he said, almost whispering.

"But why?" the cries went up. "How did she die?"

"It looks like the poor woman hadn't eaten all the time she was here, and her strength was depleted by exhaustion."

"No, it's not right," the people protested. "We offered to pay her."

The widow shouted, "I offered to cook her a meal."

The mothers added, "We wanted to given her some food."

Person after person shouted his or her offer that the woman had refused.

The doctor held up his hands, and the crowd became quiet. "You still don't understand, do you? Everything you offered was payment. It is not that you were not grateful. It is just that you could not accept the gift. You had to compensate her for what she gave and did. She would have accepted what you offered if you would have given it as a gift. That is the tragedy of this whole experience. She did not want to be paid. She wanted your gift."

"But who was she?" a man called from the back of the crowd.

"We never even knew her name," another person shouted.

The doctor let his eyes slowly scan the faces of the townspeople in front of him. He knew every one of them; some of them he had brought into the world. "I know who she was. She told me her name just before she died. Her name was Grace."

Prayer

I am so good at giving but receiving makes me very uncomfortable. Whenever someone does something for me, I think that I am obligated to him or her. I must fight the

*urge to repay the kindness. But then, it isn't a gift anymore,
is it? Teach me to say the simple "Thank you!" and to
accept the gift in the spirit with which it is given. And
thank you, Lord, for your gift of grace. I pray I can receive
it graciously and use it wisely. Amen.*

A Pilgrim's Journal

- Are you a good giver or good receiver? Why do you think you are the way you are?

- When did someone feel obligated to return a gift of kindness by doing something for you? What does that do to the concept of giving?

- God's grace has been defined as a gift given with "no strings attached." What are some of the strings we attach to God's gift?

The Window

ONESTLY, I DON'T KNOW WHAT I AM GOING to do with that girl, Sally's mother thought. She is never around when I need her. It's not that she doesn't know that I can use her help. And I've spoken with her about this often. Things would be much easier if she would just cooperate a little. I get so tired of having to ask all of the time. A mother shouldn't have to ask. Oh sure, she's told me often enough that if I need her I should call. But it shouldn't have to be that way. I get tired of asking all of the time. Just once I would like her to come to me and ask, "Is there anything I can do to help, mother?" Is that really expecting too much?

"Sally....Sally, where are you?"

"Up here in my room, mother," called a voice from upstairs.

Just as I thought. I don't know what she does up there. I've asked her often, but all she says is, "Oh, nothing." How can anyone spend all that time doing nothing? She sits up there in her room, looking out the window. So much more would be accomplished if she would get down here and help by washing the pile of dishes that was left in the sink.

Sally moved away from her bedroom window. "Goodbye, little ones," she said to the nestlings as they hungrily searched for signs of their parents and the next meal. "I've got to go now."

I guess I am in trouble again, Sally thought. I can tell by the tone of mother's voice that she's upset with me. She knows where I am. I'm always here.

Poor mother. She's always so busy. It's been a long time since I've seen her happy or seen her enjoy herself. It hasn't been easy for her, with Daddy away so much with his work. I guess everything falls on her shoulders. I just wish she'd take a minute or two and sit with me here and look out my window.

She's missed so much by not taking time to look out my window. I can see the whole world from here. In the morning I can watch as the sun starts to peek from behind the mountains. At night I look up and see the sky, just like a ceiling over the earth, filled with millions of tiny, bright, sparkling lights. I've watched as Mr. and Mrs. Robin built the nest in the tree next to my window, and now they have small blue eggs that they keep warm. It is so interesting to see how they now take care of their little children. I hope to be here when the small birds fly for the first time.

Oh, there is so much to see and learn. I like to watch the neighbor's children as they play. So many of their games will be preparing them for the future. And off in the distance, I can watch the cars going up and down the highway. I often wonder about the people in the cars: who they are, where they are going, and whether they are happy or sad. I sometimes make up stories about them, and I wonder if I am right.

I never get tired of looking out of my window. It is never the same. What I see is always changing: the snow falling in winter, trees budding in spring, flowers blooming in summer, bright colored leaves falling to the ground in the fall, people walking by our house, sheets of rain that

turn into a summer storm, powerful flashes of lightning
reaching from high in the sky down to the ground, and all
of the creatures large and small. As I look out my window,
I see how beautiful God's creations are. And sometimes
when I look out of my window I see my own reflection,
and I know that I am a part of all of that—I am also
something that God has made and now loves.

"Sally! Sally Ann!" Sally's mother's voice interrupted
her daughter's thoughts.

"I'm coming, mother," Sally answered as she took one
more look out of the window before leaving her room and
going downstairs to her mother.

"Sally, what in the world were you doing up in your
room all that time?"

Sally wanted to tell her mother about the baby birds
and the neighbor's children, the sun, stars, and rushing
cars, the people who walk by their house, the snow, buds,
flowers, and leaves, the rain and lightning, and the
creatures large and small. But most of all, she wanted to
tell her mother about what she thought when she saw her
own reflection in the window, but she didn't. All she said
was, "Oh, nothing. I was just looking out of my window."

Prayer

*Lord, your friend, Mary, took delight to sit at your feet and
be fed with the spiritual food you gave her while Martha
fussed with so much activity. I am like Martha: working all
the time just to keep busy. I need to sit down—be silent and
still—and listen. They are the better things. Be patient as I
learn that an activity for its own sake will not have rewards
but instead just wear me out. I want to sit at your feet and
be fed also—fed with the sweet-tasting words of life and
love. Amen.*

A Pilgrim's Journal

- Why do you fill your life with so much activity? Make a covenant with yourself to take time to be still and listen.

- What wonders of God's hands do you enjoy watching and meditating upon?

- Light a candle and listen to its message. Remember, Jesus said that he is the light of the world. What new wonders did the candle reveal to you?

A Day at the Clinic

HE LARGE AMOUNT OF PEOPLE WAS almost too much for Pete. This many bodies in such a small room awakened his long-forgotten phobia. Ever since he had started his corporate climb, he had been able to distance himself from uncomfortable encounters. He had gained his status by knowing which people to cultivate and which ones to neglect. It meant little to him that those whom he left behind resented his attitudes. They felt used, and they had been!

"What am I doing here?" he asked himself. "This is not going to do a thing for my image. Why did I agree to come?"

The sound of a wailing baby interrupted his reverie. In the corner of the crowded room, a mother tried to soothe a tiny infant flushed with fever. The young mother's look of concern made her look older than she was. Pity tugged momentarily at Pete's heart, but the feeling did not last long. In his world, everyone got what he or she deserved. The woman's plight was the result of either missed opportunities or unfavorable environment. He banished his concern for her with the thought, She's probably not even married, anyway.

A raspy hacking cough pulled Pete's attention to another part of the room. An old man sat bundled up to ward off the unheated room's damp chill. Pete turned away in disgust when the man brought an old, soiled handkerchief to his mouth and coughed some phlegm into it.

The door opened and in walked a young man with glazed eyes. He was so thin that Pete wondered how his frail body could support any life at all. The young man appeared nervous and he was sweating profusely in spite of the room's chill. His arms were bare. Just below a tattooed eagle on his left arm, a few small, purple patches mottled his skin.

Oh great, thought Pete, just great. Here I am breathing air with the very people I have made it a point to avoid. From what I've read, that guy probably has AIDS. He's high on some drug, too, from the way he looks. Probably got AIDS from a dirty needle.

His thoughts were interrupted as Dr. Sanchez entered through the door that led to the clinic's waiting room. Pastor Wayne, for whom Pete was waiting, was there as well. "Hi Pete," Pastor Wayne called, flashing a smile. "I'm glad you could make it. To tell you the truth, I wasn't sure you would remember."

"How could I forget," Pete mumbled irritably. "You left four messages with my answering service and sent notes to my home and office."

Pastor Wayne laughed. "I guess it comes from my compulsive nature. I don't like things to get away on me. Come here and meet Dr. Sanchez. I believe you were in church the Sunday he spoke about his work here at the clinic?"

Pete remembered. How could he forget! The doctor's presentation had moved even him. But being here today had not been Pete's idea. His wife, Miriam, had thought it would be good service to the community if they both signed up to help out at the clinic. They had the means and time to do it. She had already completed her turn, and Pete found himself in a sticky situation. He had a promise to fulfill.

Dr. Sanchez was tall and walked with the stoop that is usually associated with tall people. He held out his hand to Pete, who was surprised at the gentleness of his handshake. It was firm but not overpowering. His smile was genuine but not broad. Both his eyes and his mouth projected years of hard work, pain, frustration, and devotion to his cause. Dr. Sanchez's dedication had resulted in the establishment of this clinic in the poorer section of town. He was well known in the community, and everybody accepted him. He was a reminder that the town had its serious problems.

"Well, it's time to get to work," Dr. Sanchez said in a soft voice. "Pastor Wayne, please take a few minutes to fill Pete in on what he will be doing." He turned to the young woman with the baby. "Maria, you can bring Carlos in now, and I'll take a look at him."

Pastor Wayne took Pete aside and explained the clinic's procedures. But no matter how well the tasks were explained, nothing could have prepared Pete for what was in store. An endless stream of people kept the waiting room full. He had no idea that the town held so many people in need nor was he prepared for the poverty he encountered. As the day progressed, he forgot his aversion to being there.

In fact, as the hours passed, his compassion grew. Was it the grandmother who brought in a small child who had been bitten by the rats that ran through their tenement halls during the night? Or the battered young woman who had been beaten by her husband? Or the teenage girl who feared telling her parents of her pregnancy? Or the homeless man who had a biopsy taken from his neck, which Dr. Sanchez was convinced was cancerous? Or was it the result of all of the people who together made a collage of human need?

Late that evening, when the last patient had left and the clinic was securely locked, Pete, Dr. Sanchez, and Pastor Wayne walked a few blocks to an all-night diner where they ordered their first meal of the day.

"Pete," his pastor observed, "you look preoccupied. What is it?"

"I wasn't ready for what I saw today," Pete answered. "I don't know what to do. We can't let Dr. Sanchez go on like this." He then addressed the doctor. "How can you survive this strain?"

Dr. Sanchez twisted the coffee cup in front of him on its saucer. "I really don't know myself," he said. "Even I wasn't prepared for all of this when I opened the clinic. Oh, I had some idea, but my idealism then was stronger than it is today. I guess what keeps me going is the reward of knowing that people are going to be cared for who otherwise would go untreated. Most of them can't afford to pay anything at all. Help from the public sector is so twisted up in red tape that it is almost not worth the trouble going after it. I have a practice in another part of town that helps to pay for what goes on down here. But it is what I do here that energizes me. That's how I keep going."

The three men sat in silence for what seemed a long time. Pete finally broke it. "But what can I do? What can anyone do?"

Pastor Wayne spoke softly. "Care. What you can do is care. See these people as your brothers and sisters who need your love and concern and help. Tell others the story of what you experienced today. Get some of your friends to give us some of their time and resources. Encourage them to use their connections to help get the things we need. But most of all, look upon each person as someone whom God loves as much as he loves you. You are no better or worse than they are. They deserve respect. If Christ were here today, I firmly believe, he'd be working at Dr. Sanchez's side."

Silence descended again over the trio. The waitress came and placed their platters before them. The food was hot and smelled delicious. But none of them immediately picked up the silverware.

Their minds were filled with visions of the people they had met that day.

Finally, when they had finished eating, Dr. Sanchez rose and said, "I must leave. I promised Maria I would stop by to see how little Carlos is doing. Will I see you again, Pete?"

Pete looked up into the doctor's eyes and said, "Just try to keep me away."

Prayer

Dear God, there is so much pain around me that I do not know what to do or where to begin. Surely, the little that I can offer will not ease much of humanity's anguish. But I wonder if that is an accurate assessment or just an excuse? Yes, I really do know the answer to that. You tell me that my purpose is not to ease the torment of humanity but to reach out and touch those who are near me—to be one of a whole host of servants who care and are compassionate. I do not want to be immobilized the enormity of the task but energized by your will to heal. Amen.

A Pilgrim's Journal

- When have you been moved by the plight of humanity to do something, no matter how great or small it was?

- "Compassion" means to suffer with. Who has been compassionate to you? Why? What message did that person's compassion bring to you?

- When has another person's need turned you aside from what you were doing to be the presence of Christ to her or him?

Judgment from Within

OW, AFTER ALL THOSE YEARS, THEY SAT IN the same room waiting for their appointments with Doctor Harrison. They never knew they were both seeing the same gynecologist.

What does one do in such a situation? Irene shifted her weight from one hip to the other as she tried to avoid making eye contact with Connie, who sat across the room paging through last year's collection of *People* magazine. All of the reading material was piled on the table next to Connie, so Irene—not wanting to start any conversation—stared at the swirling print in the material of her dress.

Connie slapped the dog-eared magazine onto the tabletop. "This is ridiculous," she said. "Are we going to spend our time waiting for our appointments pretending that we don't know each other? Hi, Irene. It's been a long time."

Irene was very uncomfortable. "Yes, it has," came the whispered response. Irene did not look up but gave a nervous twist to the end of her belt. Her face was flushed, and her bottom lip trembled.

More silence filled the room with awkward tension. Irene jumped when Connie asked, "How are Bill and the kids?"

"Fine." More silence. Irene rummaged through her purse, found a tissue, and dabbed at the corners of her eyes.

"Irene," Connie said. "Irene, look at me. Good God, what are we doing? There was a time when we could never be separated. People used to call us the 'Siamese Twins.' And look at us now. We can't even carry on a civil conversation. This has gone on long enough. Heavens knows, I've wanted to call you often enough, and I should have. I'm sorry."

Irene looked up with a start, as though someone had slapped her. "Oh no, Connie, please don't apologize. You're not the one to do it. I have been living in hell ever since I did that dumb thing years ago. I can't even look at you without feeling the guilt and shame of what I did. And I didn't call you because I couldn't. I did not believe you could forgive me, and I can't ask for your forgiveness now."

"But, Irene, I do forgive you. I have forgiven you. That's what makes me feel so guilty—not telling you, letting you live all these years without knowing it. Sure, I was angry at the moment. Angry and hurt. It was a terrible thing you did. But I got over it. Now the terrible thing is what I did—not telling you."

Irene's eyes were downcast again. "I'm not sure it would have done any good, Connie. I haven't been able to forgive myself. It was dumb, childish, impetuous…but it was terrible. You probably would have wasted your call. I just hope God can forgive me. I know I can't."

Shadows moved on the frosted glass of the door that separated the examining area from the waiting room.

"Looks like they're getting ready to see us," Connie observed. "Is this the way we are going to part again, with so much unresolved?"

Irene started to speak but Connie interrupted, "No, let me finish. Look at what we have done to ourselves. Look what we have put ourselves through. We have spent unnecessary time in our personal hells because you and I chose to nurse our guilt. We can free one another. I am not so naive as to think that we can start over where we have left off or erase the memory as though it never happened. But let's not hold back or reject what both of us need. Irene, forgive me...and forgive yourself."

Irene shook her head. "I don't know if I can. Oh, I can forgive you, but I am not so sure about the other part."

"Try," Connie said with a voice of authority. "Try! We've judged ourselves, and now maybe you and I need to turn a corner and let it go. Try, Irene, try for the love of God."

The door opened, and the nurse announced, "The doctor will see you now. Mrs. Wilson, you're in the room on the left. Mrs. Van Blake, to the right please."

They stood, and Connie walked over to Irene. "We owe it to one another. We owe it to ourselves. Try."

Irene nodded her head. "I'll try. But no promises."

"That's all I ask," Connie smiled. "How about we have coffee some day?"

"No, I don't think so," Irene said.

Connie nodded her head knowingly. But as she walked toward the door, she felt Irene's hand on her arm. She turned and saw the faint hint of a smile on Irene's lips as she said, "But if you make it a sundae, it's a date."

"Irene," Connie laughed, "you haven't changed a bit. You're on."

Prayer

Do we treat our sins like a kite? Let them go but make sure a string is tied firmly to them so that we can haul them back in again? Can we ever really let them go? Can we accept forgiveness by forgiving ourselves? Oh Lord, you did not die on the cross so that we would be consumed by our own guilt, but so that we will acknowledge it, confess it, release it, and repent it. In you is our liberation. Help us to be truly free. Amen.

A Pilgrim's Journal

- What baggage of guilt are you carrying that you need to release?

- If you were to write a note of pardon to someone who needs to be unburdened, what would you say?

- What images can you think of that would describe the power of forgiveness?

The Very Best Christmas Ever

HE LIGHT SNOW BARELY COVERED THE road that ran through the village of Jeddo, a small coal mining town in Pennsylvania.

"It looks like we're going to have a white Christmas after all, Mama."

Margaret wiped the smudge she had left on the window when her nose pressed against it. Her mother, Kelly O'Donnell, looked up from the popcorn she had been stringing to be used as a garland for their Christmas tree. She smiled at her daughter, but her eyes betrayed a deep sadness.

The years had not been kind to Kelly. Oh, it wasn't the birthing of children that did it. Goodness knows, they were the light of her life. Nor was it the fatigue of raising them. It wasn't even the pain of death, for on their family plot three small headstones on which rested sculptured lambs marked the graves of some of her children. It was being the wife of a coal miner that had taken its toll: the hardship, fear, and eternal debt to the coal baron from which they could not escape.

Often when Emil, her husband, received his pay, so much was deducted to pay for their "tab" at the company store and the rent for the company home in which they lived that few coins rubbed together in his pocket as he made his way home. Often he wished he could stop off at the tavern to have a beer or two with his comrades, but he knew that they could not afford it.

If it wasn't for the money Kelly earned doing the laundry for some folks who lived in town, the O'Donnell family would have often gone without food. What they did eat was surely meager—mostly weak soup and bread spread with lard.

Margaret watched her mother for a few moments. She saw the sadness that weighed heavily upon her. She would do anything to see her mother smile again—and laugh. When was the last time she had heard her laugh? As it was, Margaret helped as much as she could: looking after the younger children, cooking some of the broth, and ironing the clothing her mother washed. It often happened that Margaret stayed home from school in order to help her mother.

Margaret walked over to the stove to stir the steaming liquid. The room was filled with the sweet smell of chicken stewing in the pot and bread baking in the oven of the old combination coal and wood stove. She opened the oven door, checked the bread, and, seeing that the loaves were done, lifted the tray out using her apron as a hot pad.

"Don't they look good, Mama?" she asked. Tonight was going to be a special meal. They were going to be having the whole chicken. No weak broth for Christmas Eve. This was going to be a feast complete with homemade jam for their bread.

Kelly O'Donnell once again looked up, gave a feeble smile, and valiantly struggled to hold back the tears of her heavy heart.

Margaret was old enough to understand. It hurt her to see her mother so sad. She went to her mother, sat at her feet, and, hugging her legs, said, "It'll be all right, Mama. Just you wait and see. Everything will be just fine."

"Oh, Maggie," Kelly responded, "you are such a delight—just like a ray of sunshine on a dreary day. Your cup is always half full while mine is always half empty. I wish I could be as sure as you are. It's just that I wish that for once we could...." Her voice trailed off, never finishing the wish. She had wished for it so many times that she wondered if saying it one more time would really make any difference.

She didn't have to finish. Maggie knew. She had seen it many times. On their visits into town, she watched as her mother walked past the full plate glass windows of the stores. There wasn't more that she could do than look... and wish.

Kelly was lost in the unspoken words of her wish. How she wished that this year she could give her family some store-bought gifts: a doll that closes her eyes for little Ann, an electric train with a crossing gate that goes down for Patrick, and a pair of good shoes for Maggie. But it was not to be. As in years past, the gifts were all handmade: a rag doll made from a woolen sock, a winter cap knitted from the old sweater she had unraveled, and a gingham dress made for Maggie out of the printed flour sacks from the company store. Mr. Shaunessey at the store was good enough to set them aside so that she would have enough to make Maggie's dress. Even the tree that stood in the corner of their sparse living room was an example of their poverty. It was one of the last ones left, the one no one wanted. The man let her have it for twenty-five cents just to get it off of his lot. Her family deserved more, but she could not give them more.

The familiar sounds of Emil O'Donnell returning from his shift at the mine came from the front porch: the stomping of his heavy rubber boots, the clang of his lunch pail, and the familiar whistle to announce that he had returned.

Margaret jumped to her feet and ran to the door to welcome her daddy home. "Hurry up, Papa! Come inside and see how beautiful the tree is. I made the paper birds, Patrick and Ann cut out the snowflakes, and Mama is stringing the popcorn and...."

"Whoa there, Maggie," Emil O'Donnell laughed. "Give me a chance to step into my home. Why, you're about as excited as a firecracker on the Fourth of July."

"Oh, yes, I am," she agreed. "Everything is just so wonderful. The tree is looking beautiful, there are gifts under the tree, it is snowing, and we will be going to the candlelight service at church tonight."

But deep inside, Maggie knew the real reason for her joy. She had what was most important to her: her family, her mother and father, sister and brother, and they were together. Too many times the father of a friend would die of the coughing disease, "black lung" they called it, or lose his life or become seriously injured in an accident in the deep shafts of the mines. Many mothers would just burn out or be given to staring into space. But they were still together this Christmas. And even though the gifts were all handmade, even though it was next to impossible to fill in the empty spaces in the scrawny tree, even though their Christmas meal would pale in comparison to the feasts that would be held in the sumptuous homes of the coal barons, Maggie had what was most important.

"Yes," she said, smiling at everyone, "I just know that this is going to be the very best Christmas ever."

Prayer

I have stopped getting excited by commercialization at the time we celebrate your birth, Lord. When I do, my energies are pulled away from the important things, and if the season turns up empty, I have no one to blame but myself. I can still exercise self-control. No, what is important for me is the glory and wonder of your incarnation—that you came to live among us full of grace and truth and to be the light that no darkness can extinguish. I rejoice that we are able to be reminded each year that there still is hope. Amen.

A Pilgrim's Journal

- Remember your very best Christmas ever. What made it special?

- What role does your relationship with others (family and/or friends) play in hallowing the nativity event?

- Does the Christmas event help you look beyond yourself? Explain.

Season Index

Theme Index

Scripture Index

More Stories by James L. Henderschedt

THE LIGHT IN THE LANTERN
True Stories for Your Faith Journey

1992 Koala Award Winner!

Paper, 124 pages, 5½" x 8½", ISBN 0-89390-209-8

Award-winning author James L. Henderschedt has a gift for telling imaginative stories. This collection, linked to the lectionary, goes beyond facts to the truth of one's faith journey. Use them for personal reflection, homily preparation, or small-group work.

THE MAGIC STONE
and Other Stories for the Faith Journey

Paper, 104 pages, 5½" x 8½", ISBN 0-89390-116-4

Put the word of Scripture in context with today's lifestyles and the word becomes reality for you. Share them aloud and the word comes to life for your congregation, prayer group, or adult education class.

Call 1-800-736-7600 for current prices.
See last page for ordering information.

More Stories for Your Faith Journey

WHEN GOD BEGAN IN THE MIDDLE

Joseph J. Juknialis

Paper, 101 pages, 6" x 9", ISBN 0-89390-027-3

In this collection of stories, find out what lies "Twixt Spring and Autumn," "Why Water Lost Her Color," and meet Greta and Andy, whose mountain is "Carved Out of Love."

STORIES FOR CHRISTIAN INITIATION

Joseph J. Juknialis

Paper, 152 pages, 6" x 9", ISBN 0-89390-235-7

This collection of stories is organized around the adult catechumenate. These are not allegories; they are imaginative stories that resonate with key lectionary passages and stages of the catechumenate. Great for generating discussions. Reflections, questions, and rituals for each story will help catechumens tell their own stories.

WINTER DREAMS and Other Such Friendly Dragons

Joseph J. Juknialis

Paper, 87 pages, 6" x 9", ISBN 0-89390-010-9

"A book of fifteen gentle stories that evoke thoughts of things hoped for, of things not seen. It is a book of dramas, fairy tales and fables...dancing with images that spark into clarity old and treasured principles..."
— *Milwaukee Journal*

Call 1-800-736-7600 for current prices.
See last page for ordering information.

More Stories for Your Faith Journey

NO KIDDING, GOD, WHERE ARE YOU?
Parables of Ordinary Experience

Lou Ruoff

Paper, 106 pages, 5½" x 8½", ISBN 0-89390-141-5

The author shows you where he finds God: in a bottle of whiteout, in a hand of poker, in a game of hopscotch. These stories work effectively as homilies and as ways to find God in everyday life. To help you with your planning, they are accompanied by Scripture references according to the season of the liturgical year.

BREAKTHROUGH: Stories of Conversion

Andre Papineau

Paper, 139 pages, 5½" x 8½", ISBN 0-89390-128-8

Witness what takes place inside Papineau's characters as they change, and the stories will remind you that change, ultimately, is a positive experience. Reflections from a psychological point of view follow each section; these reflections will help you help others deal with their personal conversions.

BIBLICAL BLUES: Growing Through Setups and Letdowns

Andre Papineau

Paper, 226 pages, 5½" x 8½", ISBN 0-89390-157-1

This book of biblical stories will take you deep into your own personal recovery and transform you. The author, whose dramatic tales always have a psychological edge, addresses how people set themselves up for letdowns. Great for personal reflection and group discussions.

Call 1-800-736-7600 for current prices.
See last page for ordering information.

Stories for Groups

STORIES TO INVITE FAITH-SHARING
Experiencing the Lord Through the Seasons

Mary McEntee McGill

Paper, 128 pages, 5½" x 8½", ISBN 0-89390-230-6

Sharing our stories makes our faith journey easier. These stories are based on real life experiences that help us recognize God's presence in everyday life. Reflections and questions for group sharing can lead to personal awareness and prayer. Great for faith-sharing groups, workshops, and retreats.

LORD YOU MUST BE JOKING!
Bible Stories That Tell *Your* Story

Eugene Webb

Paper, 176 pages, 5½" x 8½", ISBN 0-89390-309-4

LEADER'S GUIDE TO *LORD, YOU MUST BE JOKING!*

John E. Barone and Eugene Webb

Paper, 80 pages, 5½" x 8½", ISBN 0-89390-310-8

People remember stories. And that's what you get in this resource from family therapist Eugene Webb. Great stories set in a biblical context, with twists that make you think — about the stories, about the bible, about your story. Reflection questions help the process. Companion leader's guide helps you use the stories in retreats for adults or youth or as supplemental activities in family and other group situations.

Order from your local bookseller, or call toll-free 1-800-736-7600, fax 1-408-287-8748, or write to:

 Resource Publications, Inc.
160 E. Virginia Street #290 - WK
San Jose, CA 95112-5876